BANGŌ

Part One

A Smuggler's Tale

Written by

Steven Beattie

And

Warren Wild

Edited by

Iain Donnelly
@ Saraswati Writing and Editing

Thank you to Mary-Jane Wild for help with the covers.

Copyright © 2025 Steven Beattie and Warren Wild All rights reserved

Preface	i
Prologue	iii
The Land of Smiles	1
One Day and Night in Bangkok	6
Pattaya Pattaya	12
A Parisian, an Italian, an Iranian, and a dead guy...	17
Amazon A Go Go	27
Fuckit (Phuket)	38
Wanna	42
The Damage Done	51
Blood Diamonds	53
Curtis Tells	57
Razor Sharp	59
Katmandontdo	63
Beware of the Sasquatch	68
The Holiest of Rivers	70
And Tonight Mathew I'm going to be ... A drug Mule	79
There ain't half been some clever bastards	84
Taiwan. Working for the CID.	87
Red sky at morning...	96
The Road to Tokyo	102
The End Game	107
Tsunami	111
Never, again.	114
London Calling	116
Amsterdam	126
Return to Oz	130
The Delhi of the Beast	135
Wonderful, Wonderful Copenhagen	148
Stealing the bag/Burning bridges	151
Pattaya Bar Girls P.I.	153
One Last Job	169
From Bombay, to Santa fe, over the hills and far away.	174
Flowery Twats	188
Going down	202
Nightmare in Narita	221
Chiba	236
Meet The Gang	245
A day in the life	277

Preface

Before we start let me set the scene.

I am Generation X and the era in which this story is told is between 2000-2012. I'd never opened a computer, and for me social media didn't exist.
My Information came from books, T.V and word of mouth.

Knowledge of the world wasn't as accessible as it is today and because of this people and institutions could get away with a lot more.

I started to write this book in Fuchu prison 2010, so why so long?
The first draft was handwritten and incomprehensible even to me so I had the options of either just forget it, go back to school to become literate, or get me best mate Woz on the job.
I also asked a shit load of my mates for help and advice.
We got there in the end and I'm well chuffed.

We wrote the book with our Lancashire dialect and phrases to give it my voice, whilst trying not to go too far and alienate you heathens from elsewhere, oh and the fucking swearing is down to a minimum.

We decided to split the book into two volumes because it was simply just too big of a story for just one. The books can get quite dark at times but we addressed this with the same humour that got me through my ordeal.

Humour was a huge part of my survival and no matter how bad things got I would use it as my lifeline to sanity.

I hope you enjoy the read as much as we enjoyed the writing and thanks for either buying, borrowing or stealing it.

R.I.P.

Iain Donnelly

Iain sadly passed away a few days after editing this book.

Thanks pal.

Prologue

The descent

Bollocks, I'm going for it.

Right, here we go, this could be my last beer and last drag of a cigarette as a free man. As I look up, it's a clear blue sky and I seriously think about asking for divine intervention. Kind of weird that I've never believed but yet, here I am, thinking about it.
Oh, the hypocrisy.

I've been smelling a rat for the last two days and my paranoia is in overdrive, and it's not helped by the fact that on previous occasions, my gut instinct has been bang on.

I walk into the hotel and take the lift to the reception which is on the second floor. So far, so good;
I go to the desk and ask the manager for my case.
He's a nice guy, I was speaking to him just the night before.
If this guy is in on it, he's a bloody good actor.
Nah, everything seems fine. It's the bag, the bag is the point of no return. Once I put my hands on that bag, I'm all in.
I'd run this scenario over and over in my head and this was the point where they'd get me. I figured that as soon as I signed for the bag, they'd all come out from nowhere and arrest me.

He gives me the bag and through gritted teeth and with a clenched arsehole, I signed for it.

Nothing.

I suddenly realised I wasn't breathing, so I gently exhaled and went to take a seat to give the suitcase a casual once over.
The luggage tag from India seems fine, no evidence of tampering.
This is good, this is good.
I'm starting to feel better now.
I check the lock.
Where's the key?
I ask the manager,
    "scuse, mate?"
No reply, so I ask him again.
    "Excuse me mate, where's the key?"
He looks clueless and says he doesn't know.
He's in on nothing.
This is going to work.
    I found the keys in the top part of the suitcase where I'd bloody left them.
Half an hour from now, I'm going to be giving it the Billy big time in Roppongi, the sin city area of Tokyo.
All that worrying and overanalysing things, watching that bloody hotel for two bastard days.
Well, once again I'm coming out on top. Everything is going to be alright.
I head towards the lift.
I press the button and hear the lift coming down.
It shatters the calm of the quiet reception area and that's when I heard the clip clop sound of official shoes coming towards me.
These footsteps belonged to more than one person and the pace of them did not seem right.
These footsteps had the sound of purpose and intent.
I looked up at the ever-decreasing numbers of the lift's

descent.

"Come on… come on!"

The sound of the lift was getting louder as it got closer, as were the footsteps. I was starting to get really tense.
The lift finally slowed as it reached my floor and the pace of the footsteps quickened.
These feet also wanted to get on the lift.
The lift finally settled with a loud clunking noise and then, in the reflection of the steel door, I saw three men in suits stood right behind me.
Uncomfortably close in the classic one in front and the other two either side behind him.
My heart was now pounding.
The doors open.
The arse starts to fall out from my world.
I still cling to the slight hope that this could be just another coincidence.

They follow me into the lift.

Is this shite as like a coincidence.
I keep up the act until the very end and politely ask.

"Are you going up or down?"
They look at each other and don't know how to respond.

I answered for them.

"I know where you're going; you're following me…
and I'm going down.

The Land of Smiles

Krung Thep Mahanakhon Amon Rattanakosin Mahinthara Ayuthaya Mahadilok Phop Noppharat Ratchathani Burirom Udomratchaniwet Mahasathan Amon Piman Awatan Sathit Sakkathattiya Witsanukam Prasit.

No, I haven't been typing with my face.

Do you know what, or to be precise, where this is? It's more commonly known as Krung Thep by the Thais and good old Bangkok to us farangs or foreigners.

The year was 2002. Me and Mad Scotty, one of my smuggling buddies, had a bet who could pronounce the full name first for 1000 baht (£15 back then). Neither of us won the bet.

Scotty died in Pattaya just before I got released; he was a top lad and such a character.

I really miss him, but that's for later.

So, how the hell did I end up in a Japanese prison? Well, after a bad breakup, I was on the whiplash trying to bone anything that I could get my hands on and drinking myself stupid every night. It doesn't take long for that to get boring, plus living in a small village, the ladies soon sussed me out for the mucky sod that I was.

Shifty, a mate of mine who I was working with, was always banging on about going to Thailand for a holiday. My heart was broken with the breakup and my back was broken from being on the line all day laying bricks.

In my then state of mind, I'd had enough of hearing about it, so I said to him.

"Right, instead of just talking about it, let's fucking do it! Get me on that plane!"

I so needed a change and when we landed, I made sure to leave all that shit behind me.

Oh my, when the doors open and you walk into the stifling midday heat of Bangkok, it literally takes your breath away.

All I want is a brew and a fag but I'm just overwhelmed by this wall of intensity. Over here, I feel like a giant, being constantly badgered by these little brown people all jostling to blag their game.

"Taxi? Hotel? Mr... Mr? Taxi for you. Special cheap... cheap! Hotel? Sexy lady?"

I manage to get my caffeine and nicotine straightener which pulls me out of the madness and I just observe, taking it all in.

"We're here... WE'RE BLOODY HERE!"

I finish up and brace myself for the inevitable madness of the taxi ride.
The traffic was chock-a-block, an absolute bloody nightmare. The odd-looking tuk tuks and all the motorbikes driving about like loons on speed, weaving in and out, through, up, over, and under. Any way possible to get where they're going.

One of the first things that strikes most of us westerners is the unintelligible number of electric cables sprawling out like a pissed spiders web just over head. It's just chaos.
It looks about as safe as tap dancing on a landmine.

We stopped at the Ambassador Hotel near to Soi 20 which is one of the many bar areas.

I had previously heard of Patpong which is an area well known for the ping-pong and Ladyboys shows but to me, it sounded like a London Soho scam type place, which it bloody well is to be honest.

Mind you, over the years, I have ventured in and have had some cracking nights there but it's not for the newbie, as we very much were.

The first time over there you stand out by a mile, with a constant look of…'What the fuck?'
Just walking down the street is a feat in itself.
You're constantly on the lookout for potholes, stray dogs, cats, monkeys, snakes, motorbikes, blaggers, and beggars, to name but a few, all the while with sweat dripping off you and constantly saying,

"Fuck me, it's hot"
as you walk past workers wearing balaclava hats like a crap Spiderman with jumpers on.

Walking round the food stalls and bug trucks with a constant grimace as I watch in amazement that these creatures can be eaten.

Elephants on the scrounge;
big, fuck off elephants, walking up and down with their master on the blag.

I even saw a big crowd screaming and shouting like the Russian roulette scene from The Deer Hunter, all gathered around a steel bin betting on who would win between a hedgehog and a rat.
The Hedgehog won on points… ba-dum tss.
What is weird is the fact that over the years, you get used to it.

Trying out all these new foods was a challenge.

The first real hot dish I tried was when I was sat at a bar watching the girls eating what looked like green beans in a thin-looking soup.

One girl said,

"Hey, you want try?"

"Is it hot?" I asked.

"Sapicy, nit noi."

"What?"

In a charades-type gesture for small, she replied,

"little, little."

So, Mr. Naïve here had a go.

I remember putting it in my mouth and straight away the brain sensing danger telling the mouth, 'EJECT! EJECT!' as my eyes widened in alarm, the girl shouted over,

"TRY, NOT DIE."

Which roughly translates as,

"Have a go ye soft git, it won't bloody kill ya."

As soon as I crunched into it, a feeling of dread spread across my whole body. I quickly spat it out.

All the girls were laughing; the old ones are the best, I guess.
To them, it really wasn't hot at all, but for me?
Not only was my gob on fire and my head visibly glowing, somehow my knees got in on it like when you get a good kick in the balls and it goes through your whole body.
Well, this was the chilli version of that.

The girls were all laughing hysterically at my performance and proved there was more than one way of having a farang's pants down.

The girls, oh the girls.

By now we all know about Thai Women. There is so much information nowadays on YouTube and social media etc. but back then, it was all new, very new.
Before going there, I had heard all the usual stories and it did sound very sad that these poor girls, mostly underage, would be forced into prostitution or trafficked somehow and fat, old repulsive westerners would be abusing these poor young girls for a pittance.
Now I'm not saying that it doesn't happen, but I am saying that I haven't seen it in all the years I've been there.
What I was beginning to see, were these very strong, independent women.
Sexy, hot, and very mischievous, using their wits and cunning to blag every last penny out of you in the most enjoyable way known to man.

They were the masters of spotting fresh meat, the first timer,
and in this case, that was me.

One Day and Night in Bangkok

Murray Head sang about the devil walking next to him in Bangkok.
Well, we took him on the piss and got him shitfaced.

The plan was to go and have a little shop at the floating market and visit some temples. We really did set off with the best intentions which lasted all of the five minutes it took to walk to the first bar.
Soi 20 was a short but sweaty walk to a complex of about 30 bars.
In the first bar, we got the full treatment of two girls each as we chatted to the Mama San (woman boss who looks after the girls) which is also ironically a Japanese word.
One girl was massaging the head and shoulders while the other would open a new ice pack and a small towel and then, starting on your face, she would slowly cool you down.
It was bliss.
We answered all their questions.

"Where you from?"
"How old you?"
"How long stay?"

All they are doing is sussing you out, weighing you up. The girls really do have a good sense of humour though, and I don't know why but I never expected that. Once the role play was over and they had recited their scripted inquiry it was a case of…

"Solly, I sa peak little Englid."

"You want play game?"

"Pool? Dice? Jenga?"

And my favourite….

"Connect Four?"

You see, the idea of these games is for them to make money without the problem of the language barrier.
They're not too good when it comes to formal chitchat and the conversation soon dries up, so in order for you to spend more time with them, they play these games. Games they're good at and usually win, and when they win you buy them a drink, a lady drink, which they get a percentage of, and this is how they make their money.
If you didn't play, it was thought of as rude or 'Cheap Charlie' as they would call it.

So, a drink they got and as I'm sat there thinking this is bloody marvellous, then the cherry on the cake strode into the bar.

Ok, picture this.
In walks the coolest ever Thai guy, complete with a trilby hat and shades with a big open suitcase in front of him, just like the scene from Pulp Fiction when the suitcase opens and this mysterious golden light comes shining out, but you never get to find out what's in the bloody thing.
Well, this is The Bangkok Magic Man, mama!
Not only is he giving you a private little show, he's selling you the tricks. In other words, for a price you get to know how it's all done.

The crazy fool would be kicked out of the magic circle if they heard of this, but I didn't care. I bought as much magic as I could carry...GET IN.

Now I will be the magic man back home in the local boozer.

So, here I was with a bag full of magic, in total heaven drinking the newfound beer of the gods, Chang daft (draught). All the while, I was having my head and shoulders massaged by one lass while another 'lady' who, after giving me the cool down, was now hand-feeding me some unknown exotic fruit whilst...Hmmm,

there is no polite way to put this ...Wanking me off!

Next stop... a BJ bar.

Let's just say it does exactly what it says on the tin.

I've barely been here an hour and already I've got a full bag of magic and an empty sack for Christ's sake.

That was me, hooked from the off.

We had a bit of a walk about with plenty of beer stops, but that combined with the heat and jet lag was taking its toll and we started to flag a bit.

We came across some girl who was drinking from a small brown bottle, and I asked what it was.

"Lipo," she said, "good for boom boom."

And all the while, she was doing that jiggy, jiggy, hump dance thing.

"Same, same, wed bull."

Lipo is a stronger version of Red Bull which was also invented in Thailand and has been banned in many countries, so it was a couple of Vodka Lipo's and...BOOM FUCKING BOOM! I'm jiggy jiggy and back in the game.

Next stop...

NANA PLAZA.

We met some Irish lads on the plane, and they had told us all about Nana Plaza and it sounded like fun, and boy were they right.

We started at a bar called Stumble Inn which is right on the corner, just before the entrance of the Plaza and still one of my all-time favourite places to chill and have a cold beer whilst people watching and eating street food.

The dishes are passed up to us from the vendors below where BBQ meats of all kinds, and I do mean all kinds, are for sale. Sometimes it's best not to ask.

I mean, once you realise you're eating chicken arse or intestines, it really doesn't go down that well.

The chicken, pork, or fish ball soup is spot on and, for the price of about 30p, you just can't beat it. You can also you add your own chillies, sugar, and fish sauce, so, there was none of the old, "sapicy, nit noi" bollocks.

It was about 6pm by then and it was starting to get dark, and that's when the night-time ladies, gentlemen, and inbetweeners start to come in.

Most of them are dropped off by their husbands or boyfriends; the men really don't give a shit what goes on as long as the beer money is coming in.

"Money number one!"

Nana Plaza is three floors of mainly Go-Go bars where I got the impression that half of the staff were outside dragging you in.

Angel Witch was the first Go-Go bar we tried and what an eye opener that was.

When we arrived, we were greeted with a full-on lesbian show. What I didn't know then was that this place was one of the few that really did put an effort into their act.

This was choreographed, erotic art, and I just sat there with a reyt bonk on.

Yep, we got lucky there but to be honest, I never really liked the Go-Go bars. It's very impersonal, expensive, and too bloody loud and not my style of music at all.
It's that shite, corny, dance music stuff.
I want my lesbians to be doing their stuff to cool music such as Tool etc.

Nana is a fairly big complex but there are one or two points where you have to navigate past the ladyboys.

Now then, let me tell you a little bit about these delightful predators.
They can smell fresh meat from a mile away and once they get your scent, they are all over you. They'll be rubbing your cock, arse, pretty much every part of your anatomy, and all the while you're thinking, *am I being robbed?*

The first time I had to run the gauntlet past this lot it was quite intimidating and although it's all good-natured humour, its bloody scary.

We ended up in a bar on the top floor playing drinking games with about five girls, all wearing skin-tight hot pants. Truly a sight I'll never forget and that was it, enough was enough.
Time to taste these new fruits, these exotic, erotic little brown fruits, and why have one when you can have two or fuck it… All five?
Yep, she was right.
"Wed bull" may give you wings but Vodka Lipo gives you the fucking horn.

A bloody mad and marvellous one day & night in Bangkok and not a chess board in sight.
I have no idea where Murray Head went but the devil and I

were spent, and our pockets and balls were empty.

Oh, one last taste of madness.

The tuk tuk driver on the way back to the hotel was off his head pulling wheelies, skidding, and hitting bumps just to give us a final adrenaline hit.

Wow.

Could this hedonistic trip get any crazier?

Absofuckinglutely!

Next stop?

PATTAYA!

PATTAYA PATTAYA

Remember the cartoon Wacky Races with Dick Dastardly and Muttley?

Well, imagine one of them being totally mental and on yaba (a mix of methamphetamine and caffeine popular in Thailand) and he's your taxi driver for the next two to three hours.

On this manic drive, I would be witness to the craziest of things.

Animals, humans, just about anything that walks or crawls crammed into anything that has wheels and an engine, and all...somehow...travelling along the motorway.

Destination?
One of the few places in the world that rightly deserves the title 'Sin City'.

Pattaya.

Back home, I'd heard about a guy called Pete from a neighbouring village who could get us on super-cheap, dodgy, business class flights and on my first visit here, I'd arranged to meet him.

Now, other than the odd night in 'The Drunk Tank', I'd never broken the law, so I was a little bit sceptical and unsure as to what this was all about. But, to the carrot I went.

We met Pete at 'Arrys Bar on Beach Road next to our hotel, The Charming Inn on Soi 4.

Now then, this was the point where I was starting to suss what Soi meant.

On the way to our hotel, the taxi driver seemed to be a bit lost and then, as we went down another street, he started doing a really naughty type laugh complete with Carry On Camping style eyebrows giving it,

"Ho, Ho, Soi 6."

We had absolutely no idea what he was on about but just looking at the street, you could see it was a one of 'those' types of street.

That's it;

Soi means street!

"Oreyt lads, How the cockin' hell are ya, fancy a beer?" asked Pete.
Now, before we carry on, this isn't a typo.
Pete's Dad never swore but always said "cockin'" and Pete had obviously picked this up as a kid. It always made me smile when he said it because he sounded like an old fella.
Now ordinarily, I was never one for day drinking on holiday.
It was a self-made, sensible rule that I always stuck to.
I loved to go out adventuring and getting to know the real place that I would be in.
Even at 17, on my first lads' holiday to Majorca with a bunch of mates, I was the same. They would just sit around the pool all day getting leathered while I was off, up into the hills doing my David Attenborough bit looking for snakes, lizards, and insects etc. Lifting rocks and not knowing what was under them was always a real buzz for me but alas, no plan survives contact with the enemy and Thailand is definitely the enemy of best laid plans.

'Fuck, it you only live once,' becomes a kind of mantra in this land of hedonism.

"I'll have a Chang, Pete...cheers."

And that was it, I was on the piss for the next seven glorious years.

Over the next few beers, I got to know Pete and we got on well. We had that same daft, sarcastic northern sense of humour and a few mutual friends back home.

So, after a few days of being on the lash with him, I felt I had to tell him that I kind of knew him from back home... but not in a good way.

A couple of years previously in England, Pete came over to my village and got involved in a big western-style brawl, complete with chairs, tables, the whole shebang, and he got glassed in the neck and very nearly bled out and died.

Well, I felt that I had to tell him that it was my mate that glassed him.

In the aftermath of the incident, it became a gang vs. gang revenge feud type thing.

Now don't get me wrong, this is not some tough war between the Crips and the Bloods type nonsense. It's just neighbouring towns, or in our case villages, having a scrap that got out of hand. I figured Pete, like many from out of town, had possibly only heard of me through the nickname, 'Damage'... if at all.

He ended up going on the run to Thailand over some, shall we say, misplaced ecstasy tablets. About 10,000 of the fuckers from a Manchester gang and they suspected Pete.

Not only did they want them back, but they wanted to put a cap in his bottom or some American thing like that.

With the dosh he made from nicking the E's, Pete was offski, and as a result, the beef between us lot was done.

So, there I was in 'Arry's bar just trying to get my head around everything.
I'd only been in there for a couple of hours and in that short time, I got to hear of six deaths that had just happened that day.

I was like,

"What kind of a fucking madhouse have I come to?"

A guy came into the bar saying,

"Jesus H Christ, there has just been a bad bike accident down the road."

Two young foreign silly twats had been Billy big-timing it down Beach Road on some kinda superbikes the wrong bloody way, and ploughed into two poor innocent street vendors who were just crossing the road.
We've all done silly stuff like that I guess but it seems so harsh and such a waste.
No malicious intent of course, but in the end, all four dead.

Then another guy told me that an Australian mate he knew had joined 'The Pattaya Flying Club. I asked him what it was, presuming that this wasn't the kind of club I would particularly want to join.

He told me that basically, it's a case of someone blowing all their money and losing everything (including their marbles) and then throwing themselves over a balcony, or…
someone has thrown the poor sod over a balcony to gain everything they own.
Either way, the poor pilot in the precarious position ended up in a bloody puddle on the floor. To top it all off, a German fella had plugged himself into the electric mains and… auf wiedersehen.

Meanwhile, whilst in the middle all of this information overload I was being… bloody hell, I still don't know how to describe it any better… other than… wanked off.

Yes, the new norm.
Being hand-fed, massaged, and wanked off in your shorts whilst chatting shite to ye mates.

Between Arry's and the Peacock bar, which would become my locals, there was a door at the back with what looked like Chinese or Japanese writing on it.
I didn't know what language it was, just that it looked different from all the Thai writing and more like the Chinese take-away back home.

Every now and then, we would nip in to escape from the heat and enjoy the A/C to cool down but we never felt welcome and got the feeling that they were thinking,

'What are you guys doing in here? It's not for you, drink and leave.'

The girls were also cold which in an odd way made them more attractive as opposed to the other girls who screamed that they loved you all the time.

We always want what we can't have, human nature I suppose.
We're an odd lot.

This was a Japanese bar and the first time hearing the word...

YAKUZA.

A Parisian, an Italian, an Iranian, and a dead guy…

Over time and after a bit of back and forth to Thailand, the addiction was starting to take hold, and I was starting to become part of a small community. A band of brothers, so to speak, with members from all over the world who were here for different reasons, yet we were all singing from the same hymn sheet.

French Joe was a real slimy looking twat. Some say character, I say twat.
A small, tanned Parisian with googly eyes. He never smiled and was constantly on the lookout for anyone he'd recently screwed over in the past and also always on the hunt for his next victim.
He was always up and down from bar to bar, arguing with staff over the bill, over the girl, over the heat, you name it. He had as the Thais would say, a 'plom plem (a problem).
He was like a fly on shit.
Always jumping around from bar to bar, never settling in one place. I never liked him from the off and rightly so, as my spider senses were bang on with this fucker.
I called him Kermit the cunt, not just because he was French, had googly eyes, and was a right cunt, it was…well…

well, actually, that's EXACTLY why I named him Kermit the Cunt.

Italian Alex was becoming a good mate, 'one of the lads'. It was strange, he was a bit like the runt of the litter and had a bit of the victim about him, but we took him in.
His English was pretty bad, but he somehow got our sense of humour and banter-wise, he would certainly give as much as he got.
Now, I don't know what personal demons he had.
Like many in The Land of Smiles, he was here to forget his problems and not speak of them.
That's the thing about Thailand; it's not like home where you unload all your troubles off on your mates. Here, you have a good crack and keep all that shit to yourself. Yet, you could see he was on the run from whatever his problems were.
He ended up, surprise, surprise, falling in love with a Thai girl. She was a friend of mine, a good friend of mine... a good shag. Well that was it, he wasn't going back.

It doesn't take long for the money to dry up, especially when you have a girlfriend and even more so when she's…

'Not a bar girl'.

'Doesn't want you for your money'.

and…

'I take care you, becod you hab good heart'.

Yeah, they cost the most.

Before long, it was looking like he's next in line to join The Pattaya Flying Club.
Me and Pete were helping him out with a bit of money here and there, but it soon got to the stage where it was a bit like he was taking the piss, so we said:

"Alex, mate, it's time to go home."

He had a good trade as a tiler back in Milan and could earn a decent amount in a relatively short time but no, his head had gone and he would rather starve on the beach than go home and face his reality.
How stupid could he be? Well, I know the answer...

VERY.

French Joe, "I have some good friends that may help with your Alex problem… no?"

He'd overheard me and Pete having a whinge about how to help him or get him back home.

"Go on Kermit, watcha got?"

"I'm going to meet up with a friend of mine in Soi 8 later on and he's always on the lookout for good, efficient couriers to deliver a little bit of 'chocolate' to Europe from Nepal. Hey, nothing too crazy or dangerous of course, and it could help with your Alex situation, no? I mean, he either gets the money or gets a little jail, either way he's out of your hands."

Forever 'Kermit the Cunt'.

A cunt?

Maybe, but at the time he did seem to have the solution and it was a better option than Alex ending up dead on the beach or joining the infamous flying club.

So, Iranians? Iran?

Wtf did I know about them back then?

The embassy siege thing in 1980 was the first I'd heard of Iranians. I remember watching the Embassy snooker final with my Mum and Dad.
We only had three TV Channels back then, so the snooker final was a big family event.

The next thing, a newsflash came on and the SAS were storming the place like real life action men, abseiling down the front of a big white building and throwing hand grenades all over the show.

So, apart from all the hostage situation type news, I knew very little of Iranians and to be brutally honest, I just had them all down as Middle Eastern, don't trust these fuckers, Arab types.
A very naïve and media-fed view but I'm simply and sadly recalling how I thought of them back then. What I did know was that I wanted nowt to do with them because it was never going to end well.

"Fuck this, Pete," I told him.

"You're doing well with the flights and I've a good job back in the UK so let's not get involved in any of this bollocks!"

Its ok smuggling the cigs, steroids, and Viagra, but this chocolate (Cannabis. Yes, I did have to ask) is on a very different level. To me, cannabis, heroin, coke, and ecstasy were all in that same league of 100 years plus or hanging from a rope.

I wanted nowt to do with it, but Pete, being more used to the lifestyle of dodgy drug deals, wasn't fazed at all, or didn't show it.

These are those sliding doors moments.

The go left or go right moments.

Those moments in life where one split-second decision can affect the rest of your entire life.

I went left to the Full Moon Bar where I would be, I can still only describe it as... ye get the drift, and Pete went right to meet the Iranians.

I finished my holiday and went back to the cold, rain,

bricks, blocks, mortar, bosses and dossers. The harsh reality of working my balls off just to get back to the heat, bliss, giggling my tits off, don't give a fuck and oh yeah... SHAGGING. As far away from reality as I could be, ASAP.

So, on my return, I heard that Alex was OK.
His 'chocolate; run had been a success. He got through no problem and had also got his shit together. One or two others had done it too and said it really was a piece of piss.

They had it all sussed at Kathmandu Airport because apparently, some guys on the inside would get it through... 100%.

BOLLOCKS!

Eee... ye can't beat the good old 100%.

And...

'Even if you're caught in Europe, it's only a slap on the wrist'.

Hmmm... I was still far from convinced.

I was with Walshy, who was a best mate from back home and Curtis, who was a nice, quiet, respectable lad from New Zealand in his late 20s.
We were sat chatting about all this drug running scenario and were saying how you must be fucking nuts to do that when Curtis said quite casually,

"I'm thinking of having go."

"WHAT? Fuuuuck that, mate! Don't be an idiot. Why for fuck's sake?"

I mean, this lad was far from dumb. In fact, he had a good education and had a well-paid bank job back in Wellington. He wasn't there to escape his past. He had no ex-wife, or girlfriend dramas to use as an excuse like some dickheads (i.e., ME) might use in the future.

So why?

I'll tell you why. He loved smoking the bloody stuff.

He'd stay in his room for days on end getting high as a kite with his Thai/Japanese hooker girl he had on the go. She was basically a Geisha who worked for the Yakuza at the Karaoke bar. She was very seductive and came complete with a dragon tattoo from tit to toe.

On this very rare occasion, me and Walshy acted as the voice of reason. I tried my utmost to talk him out of it.

"Just because these other bellends got away with it doesn't mean that you will. Odds on that sooner or later, someone will get caught and that could be you, ye daft twat!"

So, he took our wise words of wisdom on board, as well as himself on board the next bloody plane to Kathmandu.

As me and Walshy were flying back home together the next week, I was checking the flight path and I nudged him, pointing to the screen at Kathmandu and he just said:

"Kathmandontdo."

I replied, "Fuck that for a game of drug mules."

On my next trip back, I met up with Curtis and as much as I had tried to talk him out of it, I was eager to hear his story. He told me how it had almost gone tits up at departures in the airport.

So, this was the plan.

Normally, luggage would have to go through the scanners. But his suitcase already had the 'been scanned' tag on it and that was covered by a peel-off strip that was the same colour as the suitcase so that no one could see it. Then, the guy on the inside would take the suitcase to the toilets and remove the strip to reveal the 'been scanned' tag... TAA DAA!

So, because it would never be scanned, they could cram it full of cannabis, about five or six kilos of the stuff.
No need for secret compartments and all that bollocks.

'What about when they land?' I hear you cry.

Fear not, dear reader, they have all this in hand.
They would only book flights with the, of course, '100%' knowledge that there would be no customs at the other end. Genius. What could possibly go wrong?

The night before he flew, Curtis said he had a very strange, lucid dream or maybe something even weirder.
Spiritual? a warning from the grave?

Now, I don't believe in any of that ghost or medium stuff but what's important here is **he** did and that's all that counts. He was laid there on the bed going through it all. Stoned, of course, in an attempt to get some well-needed sleep for the long stressful day to come.

Then, the figure of an old man appeared and sat at the end of his bed and oddly, this didn't scare him. It was his grandad who had passed on earlier that year.

"Don't do it, lad, please Curtis, don't go. The wrong man will come to you. Don't go to the man in red with a beard. Please Curtis, don't go. Your mother couldn't take the loss. DO... NOT... GO."

Over and over, different versions of the same warning. Curtis woke with a bolt and a sharp intake of breath.

"Jeeez... what the bloody 'ell? Was that a dream?"

Was he that stoned? Or was it truly an apparition? Whatever it was, it freaked him the fuck out.
So, after showering and of course a good old wake and bake, he attempted to think it through logically.

As cool and nonchalant as he was attempting to appear, on the inside, he was a nervous wreck.

He was well aware how fucking ridiculous this whole thing was. Of course, he's gonna have bad dreams. He loved his Granddad to bits and the shame of him knowing what he was up to would have been heart-breaking. Not to mention his mum, dad, and the rest of his well-respected family back home in Wellington.

This was just his subconscious giving him a tap on the shoulder. Of course, it was a dream.

One last joint and then off to the airport, feeling way more confident in the cold light of day.

The guy he was to meet would come to him at the middle entrance. Curtis was a 6'4 blonde lad who stood out like a sore thumb and so, at bang on the time that was arranged Curtis felt a tap from behind and a man's voice.

"Hey mister, hey mister, I take your bag, I take good care."

As he turned around, the sickness hit him like a ton of bricks. A small, bearded man wearing a Liverpool T-shirt already had a hand on his bag.

"Please good sir, I take care."

Amongst all this chaos, he thought fast and acted on instinct, I mean, a bearded man in a red shirt? Half the buggers have beards and they're nearly always wearing either a United or a Liverpool shirt. Maybe that's why he subliminally dreamt it up. I mean, the odds of a beard and red shirt are pretty good when you look at it like that, eh?

"Are you friend of Abbie?" Curtis asked.

"Yes, yes, OK sir, very good!"

"Have you been sent to pick me up? "

"Yes, yes, no problem, sir."

As Curtis was sussing out if this was the right bloke, he

literally snatched the suitcase out of his hand and was off, confidently saying, "Follow me, good sir." Heading straight towards the baggage scanning X-ray machine.

At this point, Curtis came up with the good old plan of, FUCKING LEG IT!
Without looking back, he quick marched out and grabbed a taxi to the city to get back to the one place he felt safe: the hotel.
He was so paranoid that all the 'feds' were onto him that he zigzagged in and out of all the streets trying to lose any potential tails. He was full on living in the movie, 'The French Connection'. Trying desperately to escape whilst all the time trying to blend in. All six-foot fucking four of him.

Back at the hotel, Abbie (the man with the plan) was sat in the foyer drinking coffee, absolutely gobsmacked as to why Curtis was back so soon.

"Oh shit, what has happened?"

Curtis was in a whole world of hurt.
Whilst trying to explain to Abbie what had happened, he was worried that Abbie might be a Jekyll and Hyde type and would suddenly go off on one, thinking Curtis had bottled it and totally fucked things up.
Abbie got on the phone to the guy on the inside.

"Yes... yes... and the bag? OK… ok... failed."

So, you wanna know what happened?

Curtis fucking did.

So here it is.

The airport in Kathmandu is just full of people trying to make a quick buck. They are watching everyone and everything trying to seize on an opportunity to make some money.

The guy on the inside saw everything.
As he was walking over to Curtis to pick up the case, a Johnny-on-the-spot baggage handler looking for a tip swooped and took the case off Curtis to take it to customs, cause that's where cases go, right?
The guy has a beard and a red top. Grandad?
Curtis goes into full on LEG IT mode which in retrospect was exactly the right thing to do.
Better to only lose a case rather than a case **and** a courier.
A case can't grass anyone up.

Abbie was fine with this, and also recognized that Curtis had that look and the demeanour to be a good courier.

He tells Curtis,

"Don't worry, it's not a big problem.

Some days the pigeon, some days the statue.

You enjoy the rest of your holiday, go trekking, see Everest.

You should be out white-water rafting.

Don't worry, go and see this beautiful country."

So all the while that Curtis is thinking he's totally fucking blown it, Abbie is thinking of bigger things… JAPAN.

Amazon A Go-Go

I'd been back in The Kingdom of Thailand for about three weeks and was going through money like it was nothing, but on the plus side, an off shoot of me pissing my money away was that I was getting to know lots of new and interesting people.

One such character was Alan from Newcastle who was the owner of the Amazon A Go Go.

He'd had some bother with the locals so offered me and Karate Clive a job as security for a week or so depending on how things went.

Karate Clive was a 6.4 lunatic who was always accidently hitting people whilst dicking about doing "Karate" on 'em.

Amazon was one of the smaller go-go bars down walking street, known affectionately as "wanking street" and had its own, very unique shows.

The standard for a Go Go bar is 20 to 30 scantily clad ladies dancing on poles with some kind of cabaret show thrown in, but here, twice a night a charming woman in her 40s would come out and do some kind of tribal dance.

Now, do you remember the movie King Kong when all the natives would do all that tribal dancing around the starlet who was to be sacrificed to Kong?

Well, it was like that but really shit.

You just knew she was going to do something extravagant such as firing ping pong balls out of her fanny or pulling out razor blades on a string a la sticky Vicky from Benidorm.

Or, and I'm only saying this because I've seen this done before, maybe, she would stick a paint brush up her flue and do some kind of artwork, or write your name in the hope that you would pay for her talent via a bit of a scam where they would ask you your name then she would do her magic and say,

"look this is for you, $5 Steven."

"FUCK... OFF!"

One thing for sure is she couldn't dance for shit and wasn't the best looker either.

So, let's just transport you there, back in time to this momentous occasion.

There she is wildly flailing around doing all her tribal dancing then, the music drops, and we're left with just a low jungle drum beat.

DUM DA DUM DUM, DUM DA DUM DUM.

This goes on for a minute or so, all the while building up the tension.

The music would start to get louder and louder.

I didn't know what was gonna happen, at one point I was half expecting some bloke to run out in a gorilla suit and give her one.

Onto the big finale and it all built up to this "spectacular" crescendo where she would squat down and let out this blood curdling scream.

And out plopped.... a giant bull frog!

I've got to say I didn't see that coming.

I mean, bloody hell.

How the fuck does she come up with that idea?

You can almost imagine her going through a list of creatures that would leave the audience astounded and amazed after witnessing such a world beating act and saying,

'yeah, that's the one, that 'll slay 'em'.

Most Go-Go bars have a theme and I can't help wondering which came first.
Sticking the bull frog up her fanny or the name of the bar.

The frog seemed fine with it all.
I mean, it didn't try to hop off or anything. It was like,

'Well, I'm fed, taken care of, and get pussy every night.'
What would you do?   Live in a pond and eat bugs?
Fuck that.

Her second show was similar but this time the music was the Birdy Song.
I was expecting something similar to her first act. Some kind of reptile, like a salamander or maybe a small boa constrictor?
It wouldn't be anything too extreme, surely?
What can I say. It was certainly unexpected and 10/10 for originality.
What happened next dumdfounded me.

I can only describe it as her giving birth to a FUCKING PARROT!

What a very bizarre sight.

Seeing a live parakeet being birthed out of a woman's vagina. How does it breathe? I mean, I get the frogs; I can imagine them being quite happy and settled in that warm, wet, enclosed, tropical environment but a bird?

I don't know, but it never flew too far away and was on the payroll twice a night without fail like every fecker else.

I took some friends there that hadn't seen it and for a laugh, I jumped on stage, laid on my back, and let the lady drop the bullfrog on my face. (Ha... lady?)

Now of course, I expected the bullfrog but what I didn't expect or remember seeing the first time was all the juices. Was it K.Y. gel she was using as a lubricant or was it something the frog had excreted?

Fuck's sake, not frog piss…please.

Fuck knows, but whatever it was, it came dripping out of her… prior to the guest from the gash, right onto my face.

Oh my God!

I could puke just thinking about it. The things I'd do for laugh when drunk.

The job Alan offered me and Clive was perfect for two pervy piss heads.

A few days earlier, two young Thai lads had come into the club and were flashing guns around to intimidate him.

They told Alan, "We come next week and you pay 100K baht or big trouble!"

Now, Alan was pretty old school and had a few nightclubs in Thailand as well as back home in the UK. So he's no stranger to the darker side of the business and although not overly worried about these two wannabe gangsters, he asked me and Clive if we would just simply hang around the bar and in his own words, 'show a bit of a presence' so that any spying eyes could see he had foreign security on the job.

Alan had a Thai solicitor that knew a lot of 'people' and could put feelers out to find out who these guys were.
No results came back. No one had heard of them because they were just a couple of chancers.

His solicitor would soon have them dealt with by setting them up and getting them sent down.
It's all about who you know and who you can buy.
I always liked a good punch-up with the best of them but guns? No thank you, sir.
He insisted that if the lads did come back for real, we were to get out the back, and leave it to Mr. Dam (black) the only other **real** security guard in the club.

Mr. Dam was half-paralysed from a stroke and in his late 40s, but his working half was very intimidating.
He was an ex-Muay Thai champion boxer who really did have the genuine 'I could have been a contender' story.

He ended up on the piss and as a result, having a stroke. He really looked the business though, and he truly did have presence.

Bloody hell, we got some stick off the lads when we told them that we had been hired as the presence.
They could laugh all they wanted but we got free beer from 10 p.m. to 2 a.m., could take any dancer we wanted, **and** we were getting paid 20,000 baht a week.

So, we got paid £300 to drink, fuck, and look hard....
the perfect job for a couple of skint brickies.

The perfect job remained perfect for about five days as I recall, and then, like anything else the sheen started to wear off. I was sick to death of hearing the same loop of shitty pop songs over and over again and listening repeatedly to how Clive was being ripped off by his girlfriend.

To make matters worse, I didn't take any of the free love because it was at this point that I was falling for The Silverback (*All will be explained shortly*).

Also, the lads and other new friends would only come in for an hour or so and then it was off to what always seemed a better option,

"oh, we're off to a party, there's a big do on at so and so" blahblahblah,

Why is it we can't be happy with what we have?

I was trying my best to be positive and think what I **could** be doing.
Only a few weeks before, I was down in a wet muddy hole laying bricks and blocks breaking my back to get back here.

Well, what would happen next would truly put all things into perspective.

Me, Pete, and Walshy were sat in The Jack O' Tar having the crack as per. Basically ripping the shit out of each other in that typical northern fashion.

Northern humour is out on its own. To the uninitiated, it's just downright mean; really cutting to the bone and getting quite personal, but that's the thing.
Because you are best mates you can do that. It kinda reaffirms the friendship because no one else can get away with that. Weird, I know, and a lot of the other lads from different parts of the world really didn't get it and couldn't tell if we were

serious or not, but it was all just pure banter.

I can't recall as to why or what we were laughing at but I got a call and this was one phone call I'll never forget.

I was in stiches laughing from whatever it was that tickled me when I answered it.

The Phone Call

A call from home back then was extremely rare, if at all. It was one of my sisters Wendy, and straight away I knew this wasn't good.

"Steven, you need to come home soon as possible. It's mum, she's in a bad way and they say she won't last another 24hrs".

I went straight into some kind of shock and just simply couldn't reply.

"Steven? can you hear me?"

"Ste? It's Mum. Get home as soon as possible."

I just stood there...stupified.

It was as if time had just stopped, like a huge slap across the face that snatched the voice from me.

Pete could see that something was wrong and came over but I couldn't speak to him either. My eyes were glazing up with tears, I just handed him the phone whilst shaking my head and walked away.

It was too late to fly out that night but I was on the next flight the day after; it was a night I'll never forget.

My mate Baz had just come in that day and was planning to meet his online girlfriend for the first time, but on hearing the news about my Mum he didn't want to leave me, so we decided we'd all go to the restaurant where his future wife worked to meet her.

My head was smashed with worry for my Mum.
The flight had been sorted and I was just hanging around in the foyer of the hotel not knowing what to do. I really wasn't up for doing anything, but the lads were having none of it.

"There's no point just moping around worrying about it, you need to take your mind off it, you need a distraction."

Fair play to the lads for helping me through, though.

Walshy turned up with two girls on either side and said, "reyt, dude, let me sort ya out with these two."

They were really fit, proper lookers, but I just wasn't up to it. For all the good intentions, this just was not the time for anything like that.

Baz said,

"do you want me to get in the ring and have a fight with a Thai boxer for the crack?"

I replied,

"yeah go on, it might help watching you get twatted."

So, we left the hotel and set off down wanking street to where the small boxing stadium was.
When we got there, Baz went down to the ring and started talking with the fighter. It all seemed to be taking a bit too long.

I said to Walshy,

"He's fucking paying him off to take a dive so that he can look the hero in front of everyone."

So, when Baz went off to get changed for the fight, me and Jason went down to see the boxers who we already knew because I'd been in the ring with them a few times before.

I said to him,

"OK, how much has he offered to pay you off? Come on, whatever he's offered you to take a fall, we'll double it for you to twat him."

Baz had anticipated this and already scuppered our chances of scuppering him by double scuppering our scupperiness.

All we got out of the Boxers was, "cannot, cannot."

So, the fight went ahead and I'm not kidding, it was the most pathetic dive I have ever seen.

We all shouted, "FUCK OFF."

The Thai boxer looked at us as if to say, 'what I am supposed to do? He's rubbish'.

These guys take dives all of the time because the boxing in these kinds of shows is staged to make it look more exciting. You know, the big come back and all that kind of stuff, so they're really good at it but because Baz was so shit, it looked really pathetic.

We all laughed like fuck and fair play to Baz, it did help take my mind off things... Thailand's crazy mind escape to the rescue again.

The morning after, I got smashed at Arrys bar before setting off to the airport. I remember having a right old spin on while trying to sleep in the taxi.

It was the longest flight ever.

Even though I was in the luxurious business class, courtesy of 'Cyrus the virus' and sat next to some millionaire F1 team owner called Eddie Jordan (I know fuck all about F1).

We didn't chat about much; he was on about the race in Kuala Lumpur where he'd just come from, but my head was elsewhere.

My brother picked me up and we went straight to the hospital. On the way there, he explained to me what had happened.

She had a blood clot in her leg which travelled up to her heart, and she just slipped away into sleep and never woke up.

We got there half an hour too late.

I just fell back against the hospital wall and slid down it with my head in my hands sobbing uncontrollably.

To my complete surprise, the funeral was an oddly pleasant experience.
It was a humanist funeral. I'd never even heard of one never mind attend one, so that fact that my Mum's was my introduction to it was kind of nice I suppose.

My sisters did a wonderful send off and it was done in such a way that she would have appreciated, I'm sure.

Dad had passed on three years before and sadly had

the long-drawn-out cancer, so with Mum passing away so peacefully and not suffering it felt… well… acceptable.

They both went far too young; they were only in their early 70s and it was totally down to smoking like bloody chimneys all their lives.
Thank God times have changed and less and less people are smoking but come on. I mean, I got banged up because cannabis is illegal even though it's an actual plant and has many benefits to society, yet cigarettes are fine.

Which does the most harm to people?

FUCK YOU, governments!

Mum wasn't religious at all and rarely spoke of such things, but if there is a place for the good people of the world to go to, then she'll be there asking if anyone wants a cup of tea.

Trust me, I'm far from perfect but I can assure you that all the good traits that I have such as a good moral compass, being genuine and, believe it or not, being honest came from that truly wonderful woman.

Thank you Mum xxx

That's it.

I'm on my own now.

No one to answer to.

Fuckit (Phuket)

I got the next available flight back to the land of smiles where bad shit didn't happen. As soon as I arrived back on the scene, everyone was offering their condolences and although they all meant well and had my best interests at heart, it was not what I wanted to hear.
I had come here to forget.

Walshy knew me well and he could just see that I didn't want to hear it, not here. This is my safe place, where true love lasts forever and fairy tales happen for real.

"Come on, dude, let's fuck off down south to Fuckit or wherever that full moon bollocks is."

He never really liked the beach or the temple excursions. You know, tourist type things. But he knew I did.
A change of environment was just the tonic I needed.

The next day, we set off to get the one-hour flight to Phuket.
This was the first time I noticed that he had a drinking problem. In the morning, he was a shaking mess, just a shell of a man and he would say to me.

"Just pass us one of those vodka orange alcopops, will ya, dude?"

I'd pass him one over and he would just chug it down.
"ANOTHER."
Same again, straight down.

I kid you not, as he was downing these drinks, you could visibly see the life flooding back into him. It was as though he was a character in a drawing book and someone was colouring him in.

This was the beginning of the end for his liver.

He would end up doing a fantastic job of taking my mind off things though, as he became my poorly little plaything. He really wasn't well.

I don't know if the alcohol from his morning 'reviver' was wearing off, but he was very vulnerable and easy as fuck to take advantage of.

Just as we were walking up the stairs to board the plane, I got my ticket out and said to Walshy,

"Where's yours?"

Knowing full well that he'd left it on the table in the bar back in the terminal, and of course, I'd picked it up without saying anything to him.

Walshy replied,

"Oh shit, I've bloody left it in the bastard bar."

"Well, you best leg it and get it, you prick"

I unashamedly watched him struggle back down the stairs.

*"*Barging through families, running over children, old people **and** the handicapped".

That's how he would tell the story later but just as he was about to enter back into the terminal, I shouted,

"WALSHY," whilst waving his ticket.

Walshy stopped as he squinted his eyes to try and make out what I was waving.

"YOU TWAT."

Yes, he's an alcoholic.
Yes, he wasn't feeling very well, but fuck me, it was funny.

Because it was a short flight you only get a small noodle-style meal and as soon it was served, Walshy, still not feeling well, quickly fell asleep.
I was sat across from him and as it was a fairly quiet flight, we each got a couple of seats to ourselves. I was a bit restless and bored, so I got a couple of noodles and started to dangle them off his chin.
As there was no response to that, I proceeded to dangle more noodles out of his open mouth and down over his chest.
With all these spaghetti noodles all over his chin and chest, he looked like some kind of drunken Italian Father Christmas.
I then called over to the very hot flight attendant and explained to her that I was very concerned about the welfare of the passenger across from me.

"I think the guy in the opposite seat may have had a seizure of some kind."
She could clearly see that I was very worried about him.
She went over nervously and gently shook him awake to see if he was OK while tidying the poor sod up.
He woke up completely confused.
First looking at her, then pawing at all the noodles hanging from his mouth and down his chin.
He then turned around and looked straight at me.
I was absolutely pissing myself laughing.

" YOU TWAT."

I'm not sure if the sexy air hostess thought that was some kind of English slang for *'Thank you, kind sir'*.

This was the beginning of a series of back-and-forth banters between us on our holiday in Phuket. We had a cracking time, and I was pleasantly distracted as planned, but in the back of my mind, a seed that had been planted was starting to grow. A plan was starting to develop, and it would eventually fruit and change my life forever.

All the while we were on holiday, the dread of going back home was looming over the horizon and I was fast coming to the conclusion that I wasn't going to go back home to England.

My introduction to the world of drug smuggling had given me an option. An option to make some money without having to face reality.

As a seasoned veteran over in Thailand there were two scenarios I did not want to get involved in.

Number one: Not getting caught up with all the drug smuggling palaver and the Gangster-ites that came with it.

Number two: Falling in love with a Thai bird.

Now then, remember when I mentioned the Silverback?

Wanna

Soi 2 was a very popular area that had a really good buzz about it and some good bands played there. I often jumped up on the drums to get my rock star kicks.

They had one Go-Go bar called The Classroom and all the girls would dress as schoolies;
jeez, it really does sound a little on the pervy side, but it was just all that cringey Britney Spears look that took her to number one.
Funny that, innit?
How no one bats an eyelid when she does it but when I do it, everyone goes batshit crazy.
Just kidding, but you'll see where I'm going with this later.

It was my third visit back to Thailand when I first met Wanna at a very popular establishment called Noi Bar.
She really did stand out in a crowd.
Tall, dark, natural curly hair, and she had a bigger build than most Thai Girls; she had more of a Brazilian body.

Thailand really is a crazy place; if you look at a woman and think, *'she's really fit'*, 99.9% of the time...yep, it's a bloke.
I'm not kidding, after you've been there a while, you'll stop yourself and think,

hang on, that's a fucking fella.

On average the ladyboys are a lot better looking than the women, so cue Alan Partridge, 'I'm confused' and you can understand why so many new mongers are too.

She was constantly asked if she was a ladyboy and would respond in her best ladyboy voice which is basically someone with a deep voice trying to sound feminine.
She's the only girl I've ever met that can do this, it's really funny.

'Me no Ladyboy'.
And her favourite, the ladyboys' catchphrase,

'up the bum... no babeee'.
Then with a twinkle in her eye, she would say,

"No, I'm 100% all woman."

We hit it off straight away; not only was she attractive but she could also speak perfect English and had a wicked sense of humour. It soon went from having fun in the bar and getting to know each other to crazy drunken sex, slowing down to mad passionate love making until daylight.
Really?
Love at first night?
Maybe, maybe not, but all I knew was that I was getting drawn in and after that first night, I thought to myself,

I should stay well clear of this one.

There's a golden rule amongst us mongers, and despite my best intentions for setting off on this journey to see all the temples and have jungle adventures whilst searching for that mythical beach, I had become exactly that…

A monger.

A SEX TOURIST.

Oh, the shame.
Not really, I'm just being straight up. Anyway, the mongers' golden rule, never to be broken is-

don't have a girl longer than three days.

Any longer than that and they would more than literally suck you in. They would really impose themselves upon you and start to become a real pain in the arse.
They'd leave things in your room such as toothbrushes, necklaces, or knickers. Anything to give them a reason to go back to your place and then they would work their charm on you and you could end up genuinely falling for them and give them the chance of money, the easy life, and of course love...

Bollocks!

So, I left it a week or so before I went back to visit her.

I had distracted myself with other girls to keep my mind clear and stick to the rule, but all the while knowing that the other girls weren't as good as Wanna.

She had given me the itch and I wanted to scratch.

She could be super cool at times and really knew how to play the game but so did I... game on.

We had a few drinks and the chemistry was boiling over and as we got all touchy-feely, I felt it was the right time for me to play the game I had mastered.

Sometimes you're the cat and sometimes you're the mouse.

Between what is said and not meant, and what is meant and not said:

LET THE GAMES BEGIN.

"Hey, it was great to see you again but I'm going to meet up with a few friends down Walking Street."
I'm off shagging so get it while ye can, bitch.

"Oh, Ok, no problem, have a good time. I have some friends coming here later."
You either take me with you and pay what I ask for, or I fuck the next guy that comes along.

"I would love for you to come but as I told you before, I don't go with bar girls... but you're different."
I can get any girl I want and I don't pay. I'm not some old fool who's willing to give you my hard-earned money.

"Up to you."
Check…

And then she turned around and spotted some guy (most likely a previous customer) and shouted,
"HEY STUD."
Hey stud?
What happened to all that 'hello, sexy man' bollocks that all the other girls would screech out every 30 seconds? She would do everything better and in her own unique style.
I could feel this game of wits slipping away, one last roll of the dice and this was a tried and tested winner.

"Hey, I won't see you for a while, I'm going to an island to chill, not sure which... Koh Chang or maybe Phuket... you want to come?"

"I fucking hate boats, I fucking hate too much sun, I fucking hate island reggae. I love fucking, I love to fuck, pay up and let's go fuck."

Checkmate...

Game over...

Pass me the cheese.

This went on for a few months and then I got the job in the Amazon A Go-Go.
I was proper skint back then and Alan said that I could have any of the girls for free, but I really didn't want to.
There was no point kidding myself any longer, I was saving myself for Wanna. I really didn't want to fuck my chances up with her so when she finally did come to the bar, she soon found out that I hadn't been taking freebies with the girls and because I really was broke, when she did come to see me, it was for free.
There was no blagging from me not to pay and she never asked. No more games.
Were we really falling in love?
After my Mum died and me and Jason had our crazy adventure in Phuket, we went back to Pattaya.
The urge to see Wanna again was always there in the back of my mind, but I knew I was weak and in a vulnerable space.

I've seen so many men fall for the Thai girls only for it to go all wrong for many different reasons, but it rarely works out. That's the problem with us farangs, we all want to have that Thai fairytale relationship and when we get hooked, we bite down hard onto the belief that this is it, I am that rare occasion.

They swallow you whole.

I went to Soi 2, and as soon as she saw me, she came over and gave me a big, long warm cuddle, whispering in my ear,
"I'm so sorry about your mum."
Amongst all the crazy wild sex, partying, and laughs, not only did we get to know each other really well but we got to know about each other's family and all through these long conversations with each other, we also knew and understood how we had gotten to this point in our lives.

Like me, she wasn't from a broken home or from a poor family either. I would later go and meet them and work with her father and other family members in the rice fields that they owned, and in the evenings, we'd all get drunk on her uncle's rice wine.

There's one big reason why most Thai girls go working in bars that the modern world doesn't want to hear.
IT'S FUN.
These aren't girls that are sex trafficked or sex slaves. These are girls who are bored with their inherent lifestyle and want something more exciting. They'll hear all about the big city and what it has to offer from the elder girls who have made a successful life from having fun.

Growing up out in the villages there is very little to do, especially for older teenagers.

Imagine hearing about the big city and all that goes on and then seeing the older, wealthy women coming back to the village with all the gold dripping off them.
Many of the elders in the village would scoff at that kind of lifestyle but that made it look more exciting.
Wanna and her two best friends, who were all 18 at the time, went together looking for the big city adventure.
Five years later at the age of 23 (a number that follows me throughout this story), she met me.

   After the long embrace, we sat and had a couple of drinks and I could feel she wanted to tell me something.
   "What's up?" I asked.

   "OK, I have to tell you something and I'm very confused also. "

   "Hmm, OK." I wasn't sure if I wanted to hear the rest of this.

   "You see, there is this guy that came over about two months ago on honeymoon with his wife."

   "Wife?" I didn't expect or know where this was going.

   "They came in the bar almost every day and I don't know how it got like this because nothing happened. I didn't go with him, there was no wild honeymoon threesome or anything, but we kept in touch via text messaging and he has fallen in love with me. Not only that, but he's left his wife, sold his big business back home and..."

"Jesus H. Christ... what?"

"Em... well... he's coming to the bar... in one hour."

We just looked at each other and burst out laughing. It sounded so mad that a man could be so infatuated and give up so much after such a brief and non-sexual encounter.
"What do you feel for him?"

"Honestly? He's a lovely big handsome guy and I like him… oh, and also, he's loaded. But love? No. I hardly know him but he's given up everything for me and let's be honest, Ste, I've been here five fucking years; the party has to end sometime."

I truly felt happy for her, yet inside I could feel the hurt. In my heart, I felt the sickness coming. Not only had I lost my Mum but again, I was losing someone very special to me. Yep, I always said it would never happen to me but here we are.
As we embraced and said our last goodbyes, she started to cry and so did I. Then she buckled.

"Don't go, I love you," she said, "I want to be with you."

"I love you too, I but how can this work? I have no money and I have to go home soon, so how?"

"It doesn't matter," she replied, "we can work it out."

She was right, we could work it out and we did.
I went to meet the guy and explain everything. He was obviously upset but took it well. He told me how she never bullshitted him with promises of love and he even knew about me.

Honesty is hard to find in this world but in Sin City, it's extremely hard to find.

Wanna.

The bargirl, prostitute, or hooker as she would fondly call herself, was ironically the only girlfriend that never cheated on me.

Go figure.

The Damage Done

The Damage Done is a horrifying true story about Warren Fellows, a drug smuggler who was caught in Thailand. Ironically, I've been stuck with the nickname 'Damage' since I was about 14 years of age. It either came from when I had to go for brain scans after a really bad trip from taking mushrooms or Brian Damage the nut job bank robber played by Alexei Sayle in The Young Ones.
It's most likely a bit of both, but one thing for sure is it flipping stuck.

It's a small world.

I went to work bricklaying in Perth, Australia, in 2007 and on my first day there, I was having a beer in a pub and I went outside for a smoke. Two blokes were chatting away and I recognised the Lancastrian accent.

So once the other guy left, I said,

"ey up pal, werz thee from like?"

I was attempting to exaggerate my own accent and the lad of about 20 replied, "England."

I gave him a bit of a look as to say, *'ya daft twat'*.

"Well, I know that, but whereabouts, pal?"

He just stared back at me and said,

"Damage? Fuck me, is it Damage or have I gone bonkers?"

I had no idea who this kid was, but then he said he was from Billington, the village where I'm from... eh?
What's going here?

"I'm Mark, Mark Hartley. Do you know my dad? I know your niece."

So, we got chatting about back home and tried to fill in the missing bits due to the 18-year age gap.

We ended up staying in the same hostel and he was a bloody nightmare.
Always pissed up and causing some drama of one kind or another and it wasn't long before I christened him,
'Mark Hitman Hartley'.

We gave him a job working with us but that only lasted a day because he was rubbish.
Not a complete waste of time though because he left his Liverpool shirt which I confiscated and it would come in useful later.

What is pretty spooky is that only a few weeks ago as of writing this, he got sent down for a minimum of…

23 (of course) years for brutally murdering a friend of his.

Strange now to think how evil he would turn out to be but back then, we did end up as good mates and although he was a right pain in the arse, I still liked him and in way he looked up to me as a father figure.

Hmm, no wonder he ended up where he is, eh?

Blood Diamonds

The movie *Blood Diamonds* was a couple of years from hitting the big screen, so what I knew then about diamonds in Africa was a big fat zero.

Now, I can't remember who was having this conversation or how it happened. I don't even know why I was there in the first place, but I do know that Pete was chatting to one of the now many carriers.
What I do remember clearly, was that there was an opportunity to make $8,000 by smuggling 1.5 kg of diamonds out of Johannesburg in South Africa.

My ears pricked up and I was eager to hear more. I mean, diamonds? What harm could they do? Surely this was just some tax evasion thing?

"Pete, what's the crack with the Diamond thingy ma jig? I've always fancied myself as a 'bit of a Pink Panther', ya know? A James Bond bad guy, big bank jobs and all that. Haha."

I told Pete I'd actually been thinking about doing a 'little run' as they were now being called.

"Really?" Exclaimed Pete.

I had a large circle of mates who all knew what was going on but most of us had nothing to do with the drugs side of it.

We came on holiday for a few weeks, went back to work, and repeat. I was firmly one of those in Pete's eye's and never did he or anyone else involved ever ask me to smuggle narcotics of any kind.
I'd hardly broken the law previously and there had been no altercations with the police since I was 21.
I was the good guy.

Pete explained. "Well, ye get $8000 US."

"Where to and how are they smuggled out?" I asked.

"Japan," Pete replied.

"The crushed diamonds are packed tight into the handle of the suitcase and also into the extender bars, but they've fixed it so that the handle won't extend when you want to wheel the suitcase around. That way, nothing can work loose."

"What happens if you get caught?"

"No idea mate, but if it's worth 8K then it won't be a slap on the wrist."

Over the next few days, I was pondering over the whole set up. It sounded easy and safe enough.
The thought of being an international diamond smuggler sounded cool as fuck if I'm honest.

"Fuck it, Pete, I've had a good think about it and I'm up for the diamond job."
Never in my life did I ever think I would say a sentence as cool as this.

"I mean, thinking about the whole thing," I continued, "with the diamonds being crushed down, they must be industrial for machinery and stuff. I've used many a diamond tip blade to cut through walls but of course, when I tell the story later, it will be one big beautiful jewel, stolen from the

Queen of Sheba. Haha, yeah sounds like it will make a good story. I'm in."

"Are you having me on or what?"
Pete had a wry smile; he wasn't sure if was taking the piss.
I thought, *Owd on, I've got hold of the wrong end of the stick here.*
I had to ask.

"What do you mean?... Hang on, what do I mean?"
He still wasn't sure if I was on the wind up. Little did he know how naïve I still could be.

"Cockin' diamonds. As in crystal... crystal meth," he explained.

"Well, fuck me sideways! In fact, fuck me all ways. Are you taking the piss?"
I knew damn well he wasn't.

"Sod that, Pete, I'm having nowt to do wi that shite."

I was kinda gutted; in the last few days, I'd visualised the whole thing and you know what it's like when you do this.
You go all Hollywood.
I think I just stopped short of me walking in slow motion to some banging theme music.
I pictured me getting away with it and having loads of money.
WOW.
Me and Wanna could live off this for a good six months if we took it easy.
Me and Pete had a good laugh about it later.
I asked him,

"Did you not suss when I was papping on about with James Bond and The Pink fucking Panther?"

"Well, yeah, " he replied giggling his tits off.

"For a start, The Pink Panther is the name of the diamond, the jewel thief is The Phantom, ya bell end, and to be honest, you're always taking the piss so I kinda thought I'm not falling for that bollocks."

Talk about the boy who cried wolf.
Imagine if I'd not said anything and Pete went along with it because he thought I was having him on and then I inadvertently end up smuggling crystal bastard meth. Sometimes you can be just one conversation away from total disaster.
Pete added,

"Hey, Curtis is going to Japan again with chocolate and this time he needs a partner in crime." (literally)

So, in that short period of time, still carrying the thought that I could have innocently smuggled crystal meth.

Cannabis suddenly sounded like it wasn't such a bad option.

Curtis Tells

So I asked Curtis to tell me about the first time he went on his Japanese 'holiday'.
Basically, **this** suitcase was a whole different deal.
It was a Samsonite suitcase, a proper job.

What they would do is replace the wooden lining which was used to give it strength with a thin layer of cannabis resin which would fool the X-ray machine into thinking it was part of the suitcase.

When most people go on a trip, they would take a suitcase and a carry-on bag, so Curtis would take a carry-on bag as well as the suitcase to not only fit the criteria of an everyday tourist but to give him a 50/50 chance of getting the carry-on bag searched.
He knew they would hand search at least one of his luggage items and by not attracting any suspicion, it should only be a quick rummage and away you go.

Have you ever watched those 'Nothing to Declare' documentary type programmes.

There's always some clown who will turn up unprepared and customs start giving him the 'interview' where they ask them questions like:

"What's the purpose of your trip, sir?"

"How long do you intend to stay?"

"Where will you be staying?"

"What is your occupation, sir?"

All the while, they are observing your demeanour and how you reply.

A lot of the time, these goons have no plan and just stumble through their answers and because they're not prepared, they start to look guilty as fuck. Especially in countries like Japan where you are going to get questioned and they will try to trip you up.

Many countries are just basically a walk-through but not here my friend, in the land of the rising sun many a potential smuggler will not see it set.

Razor Sharp

Me and Curtis met for a beer and a good old chinwag.
It was two years since his first 'little run' to Japan and I was weighing up whether or not to do it, so I wanted to hear him go through it one more time, just for reassurance more than anything.

He told me that compared to Kathmandu airport and all the palaver there, the Japan trip was a doddle.
He had his story well-rehearsed and thankfully the plan of taking two bags worked.
They searched his carry on which was clean so that was it, off to Roppongi which was the heart of Tokyo where he met a cool Iranian guy called Kavoos (Kav).

He got paid, kicked back, and just chilled for a week as planned, then he was off back to Thailand.

This put me at ease... a bit.

So here we are now, two years later with countless runs being made by an ever-increasing pool of carriers and not just to Japan, but all over Europe, Australia, and New Zealand, and nobody had been caught.
Foolproof?... hmm.

We arranged to meet the Iranians

Me, Curtis, and Pete went to a big five-star hotel overlooking the city.

I felt we were far too exposed, and it would be too easy for an undercover copper to take photos of us plotting our devilish plans like the ones you see in the movies when the feds are onto the baddies.

I mean, just because it was going well up to this point didn't mean we weren't being watched, and here was I, right in the thick of it.
Welcome to the paranoid world of the smuggler.
Just because you're paranoid, it doesn't mean they're not out to get you.

The Iranians were fashionably late which just added to the tension, something I really didn't need.
Pete always said these guys were 'sound as a pound', so when the three amigos did turn up, I thought two of them looked dodgy as fuck.

Abbie, the boss who I had already heard about, was just as I imagined.
Slightly effeminate and had a really friendly presence about him and he instantly put you at ease, but the other two?
How can I describe them?

Well, one I presumed was a Thai minder of some sorts, he looked proper dodgy, and the other was... well...the best I can describe him as is a Colonel Gaddafi lookalike with a scar down his cheek.

The classic villain look, or for those old enough to remember, the Action Man toy with a scar on his cheek.
He was introduced as Razor.
Hmm, how fitting, I thought.

These two didn't say much, Abbie was the man with the plan and did all the talking, and to be honest, I was quite impressed with what he had to say.

The big plan.

Abbie explained:

"You will be two friends traveling together on a diving and golfing adventure. You will plan and book the diving trips ahead of the flight and we will give you the money to get all the diving gear you need.
The diving bag will be the decoy.
One kilo of the 'chocolate' will be thinly spread out in the lining of your main suitcase. Two kilos will be in the golf bag, a suit cover bag will have 500 grammes in it, and a computer bag will have another 500 grammes in it.
You will go via Taiwan and then by ferry to Okinawa. Then it's a ferry again to mainland Japan and then the bullet train up to Tokyo.
Now, you will have to go to Nepal to collect the chocolate. While you're there, you need to do all the tourist things as a cover.
Then you must come back to Thailand to change the stamp in your passport because the customs at Taiwan and Japan will red flag you if they see that you've come from Nepal.
So that's four kilos of chocolate. Three thousand Dollars per kilo... 12 thousand Dollars."

I quickly calculated in my head. That's 10 grand UK money.

Abbie was impressed with our demeanour and because we both weren't sporting any tattoos, that totally helped the situation. I realise of course, that every man and his dog have tattoos now but back then, they were a red flag and some people really do judge a book by its cover.

For example, there's a 10-man line up and only one has tattoos. Your life depends on picking the one that's done jail time.

Correct, you survived.

Abbie gave us a little sweetener of $500 each and once we were ready to commit, we would make contact again.
My God, am I really going to do this?
Have I gone batshit crazy? It wasn't that long ago I was begging Curtis not to do it and here I am, going with him! Aaargh, what the hell am I doing?
Ok, ok, let's look at my options.
Current mindset v reality.

Mindset: I can't go back and get a job, there's no work about, and what work there is, it's badly paid.
Reality: I always get a decent job and always manage to land on my feet. I've never been out of work for more than a week.
Mindset: The ex wasn't letting me see the kids so what's the point of me being there?
Reality: The point is that if I'm not there, then there's no way of sorting it out. One of the main and justified reasons for her not letting me see the kids was because I wasn't there for them.
The results are coming in...

Yep, I'm unjustifiably justified.

Let's fucking do it.

Katmandontdo

We landed at Tribhuvan International Airport and straight away, it was complete chaos.

Don Muang in Bangkok just seemed normal by comparison. It's funny how we soon adapt and things that at one point were 'Whoa, what's going on?' just become the norm.

It was a nightmare here, huge queues at immigration, people just pushing in, and the disgusting sound of men retching and spitting.
Get me out of here into the fresh air, please.

Once we got out, I could totally relate to the confusion and madness that Curtis had been subjected to on his first failed attempt.
As we were leaving the terminal to get a taxi, he showed me where it all happened. We nervously chuckled, most likely thinking the same thing; let's hope that doesn't happen again,

Beep... beep… beep… beep... beep… beep... beep... Fucking..... BEEEEEEEEEEEEEEEP.

Times that by a thousand and repeat endlessly and you might get an idea of how bloody annoying that sound can be coming from all the vehicles.

I mean, there is no logic to it when everyone is doing it.

Nobody actually pays any attention to it.
Nobody thinks, 'that's a warning so I need look out for whatever that beep was'. It's almost as though they think that beeping the horn is what makes the car go and if the car stops then you have to keep hammering away incessantly at the beepy thing... TO MAKE THE FUCKING CAR GO.

I'll tell you now, if we had been smuggling guns, there would have been a massacre and this would be a very different book.

The cattle for one don't give a flying saucer about who's beeping a horn or why because they run shit around here.
Holy cow, and do I mean that literally.
The roads are full of them, just strolling along with a slow John Wayne swagger about them like they own the place.

This was my first time in South Asia and once I had fully committed to doing the job, I decided to become like a method actor and 100% believed in my story and became the tourist I was playing. I would pack away the reality of what I was really there for into the back of my psyche until needed.

So, I was buzzing to see, smell, and feel all that this new experience had to offer.

There were loads of small roads chock-a-block with traffic, people carrying things, kids up and down like blue arsed flies. As well as the numerous cows loitering around everywhere, there were chickens, dogs, cats, and monkeys looking rabid up to the max.

All the while, we were enveloped in the bizarre aroma of sewage and vehicle fumes mixed in with the amazing scent of spices, chillies, garlic, and ginger frying away in huge woks for curries from the many little food cafes.

It reminded me of my first day in Thailand when my senses were on over-load, and I loved it.

Smix

In the two years that the little runs had been going to Kathmandu, up until his death I reckon Smix must have the record for doing successful drug runs.

He would do a run once every two months, sometimes back-to-back.
How he never got caught is beyond me, and thinking back, I can see Smix now and it makes me smile.

As I said earlier, when I did a run, I'd become a character, I'd be someone who'd blend in and who didn't attract attention.

Smix?
Well, I guess he went for an 'as if I'm smuggling drugs' look. He'd put his white John Travolta suit on, dark shades, and with a shrug of one shoulder and a cocky sniff announce,

"reyt, I'm off on a mission."
I think that because he was so blatant was the reason he was never caught.
He'd go up to the sniffer dogs at the airport and start petting them.

"Hello fella, you look like a good un, don't ya? Eh? You alright pal?... yeah... good dog."
I mean...the nerve.
The cheeky sod would even smoke in the flipping plane toilets. He told me how to do it.

"It's easy, Damage, just get a load of shite roll, stick it under the tap and get it all nice and wet, then, hold it up to the smoke alarm while constantly flushing between squirting the free scent, you know? that perfume ye can't nick."

So I thought, *reyt, I'll have a go.*
I got caught on my second drag.
BANG. BANG. BANG. On the door.

"WE KNOW YOU'RE SMOKING IN THERE, OPEN THE DOOR NOW."

I got a reyt rollicking off the stewardess and she even brought the captain to tell me off and explain how I'd endangered all the people's lives on the plane. I did my most sincere 'I'm sorry' whilst biting my lip so as not to mention that being an older plane, it still had bloody ashtrays on it.
Smix thought that Nepal was crap.
He told me, "It's a scruffy shithole with sweet FA to do."
Because the hotel and staff were all in on it, he just stayed at the free bar drinking himself silly.
I almost said into an early grave which was sadly, exactly what happened.

I really miss Smix, he was such a character.

Remember the tsunami that hit Thailand in 2004?
Well, Smix was sat in a deckchair on the beach and someone told him to be careful because tsunamis were hitting Thailand, so he got up, moved his deckchair about ten feet further back from the sea, and sat down again. Classic Smix.

Curtis and I had other plans.
On the first night, we found a huge snooker hall and next door there was what seemed to be an upstairs restaurant which featured an… erm… a show?
Let me explain.

The food was really good, soft tender lamb on the bone with fresh chapatis.
I was in curry heaven and then the lights dimmed.

Some kind of Indian-style music with a slow, seductive tempo was being played and a very beautiful couple came out from behind the curtains and started dancing very erotically, almost kissing as they swirled around to the beat, seducing each other, and you could feel the tension building up to something... oh please, no frogs.
Then suddenly, completely out of the blue, a huge shower of water came pouring down from above down onto them.
They were very scantily clad wearing quite revealing silky wear that was see through and ye could see the bloody lot.
Her nips were up like bullets, ye could see her bush for Christ's sake, and the blokes little tallywhacker.

Not quite the 'scruffy shithole with FA to do' that I was led to believe.

Beware of the Sasquatch

We spent the morning wandering around the city maze buying souvenirs to bolster the tourist story and I ended up buying a Sasquatch T-shirt for Wanna.
It was one of the many nicknames I had given her because she had massively wide feet.

I remember we were just chilling on our bed watching tennis (Wimbledon, I assume), and it was of those tense, silent bits before they serve when out from the crowd someone shouted...
'SASQUATCH'.
They obviously didn't but it bloody sounded like it.
Me and Wanna looked at each and... well, what do you think happened next?
Do you think we fell about laughing?
Nope.
Do you think we said, "how odd was that"?
Nope.
she punched me as hard as she could, giving me a dead arm and as I started to laugh, she brought out her big guns, or to be more precise, her big freaky toes.
Using her gigantic Yeti paws, she'd nip and twist, and she knew just the right spots that hurt like fuck; inner thighs were The Sasquatch's 'speciality'.

I had other charming nicknames for her;

someone once said to her,

'wow, you're so beautiful, you look like Shakira'.

I said, "more like Changkira."

She'd put on a little bit of weight and 'chang' means elephant in Thai so that went down like a French kiss at a family reunion and yes...

I got twatted.

My favourite nickname for her that I only ever used with mates, so yes, totally behind her back (I know, how noble), was The Silverback.

Until she'd had her Som Tam spicy salad fix, she would be as moody as fuck.

I'm not kidding, she was frigging addicted to the stuff.

I remember one night I'd taken her out for a meal on Valentine's Day and ordered a lovely steak. Suddenly, she saw a food vendor going by who was selling Som Tam and she was jumping up and down all excited giving me the eyes like 'can I get some'?

Really?

I've just splashed out on an expensive meal, and she wants a 50 pence fucking salad.

It had to be done otherwise I'd get the silverback treatment. Have you ever seen the big silverback gorilla behind the glass at the zoo looking all mean and moody with that 'don't fucking look at me' demeanour?

Yeah, that was Wanna when she was hungry and the reason why I never called her that to her face...

I just couldn't take the beating.

The Holiest of Rivers

We booked a three-day, two-night white water rafting adventure from the foothills of The Himalayas (which is Sanskrit for 'Where the snow lives') down The Kali Gandaki (the Mighty) River which is in the deepest gorge in the world; just getting up there was an adventure in itself.

The ten-hour journey was like something off a Top Gear special. Our minibus traversed around the most shite-inducing roads I have ever been on.
One false move and that's it...game over.

Getting stuck in off-road river crossings was something to behold and became like a team-building exercise, but once there, high up in the Tibetan part of the Himalayas, it was absolutely breathtaking, metaphorically and literally.

We had a basic lesson before we set off but we were mainly learning as we went along.
The instructors would take us through ever-increasing grades of rapids and as we gained more knowledge and our skill level increased, so did our confidence in taking on Grade IV rapids.

These were two of the most notorious rapids in the world known as Little Brother and Big Brother.

What an incredible trip it was and thankfully, the experience was shared with some amazing people.
This is not the kind of experience to be shared with the flaky and panicky type.

Here you need good solid people who remain calm under duress.

    We camped out on a white sandy beach by the river getting to know each other and building up the team spirit over a beer. Here I met a couple of people who I will never forget.

    Martin was a Catholic missionary who was in his 40s.
He told me how living in the high-flying world of banking had destroyed his soul and like many, he had turned to cocaine for the uppers and mothers ruin (gin) for downers.

"Greed is good." - Gordon Gekko.

    He told me how his life was turned upside down when he got a 'message from God' on a TV whilst in the waiting area of a brothel in the heart of Soho.
I was already thinking *fuck off* as he was telling me this, but as he continued, his story became more and more compelling.

    He told me that it wasn't like a vision of God or anything like that. I must stress that I really racked my brain trying to remember exactly what he said, but all I can recall is that the 'message' told him to go to Nairobi and to a specified computer shop where he would meet this guy.
The message actually named the guy, though I'm fucked if I can remember it, but whatever the case, the prophecy came true exactly as it was told to him.

    Now, maybe it was some elaborate con, I don't know, and maybe he left out the part where he had to pay money for his life-changing experience but the thing is, when he told me about it, I could tell that he really did believe in it and he was very convincing.

At the end of the day, it did change his life for the better, so go figure.

We both lay on the beach looking at the stars when I said,
"Eh? What? Should I tell him now?"
Martin asked,
"What's the matter? You OK?"
I told him,
"I'm getting a message. It's a very strong message. It's telling me to pass it onto you."
"No way. What's the message?"
"It's your round, get the beers in, ya tight fucker."
Not only was he a Devil dodger, he was a beer dodger too.

Our Sherpa tour guide was called Ahupathai, but we just called him Thai because it was easier, and he told us that his name means 'follow the prayer' in Nepalese.
Martin lifted his eyebrows and said,
"see?"
I leaned in and said,
"Bollocks. Coincidence."

What a cool lad Thai was. He was only about 30-years-old but had that 'wiser beyond his years' look about him.

He started out like many as a yak cattle farmer up in the mountains but said he always dreamed of being a tour guide for Mount Everest. I really did sense that he had that same spirit of adventure that I had, that he wanted more out of life and would take risks to fulfil that need.

I asked if the Nepalese called it Mount Everest and he laughed and said,
"no, we only say that to tourists".

He looked straight into my eyes and proudly called it,

"Sagarmatha. The Goddess of the Sky."

It was then that I realised how the West has just stamped its authority all over the world.
For thousands and thousands of years, the Nepalese have called it Sagarmatha then us bloody Brits come along, stick a flag in it, and now the whole world only knows it as Everest after some poncy twat.

He achieved his dream and twice made it to the top of the world. I was fascinated to hear all about it.
How he did it.
How long did it take him?
Who with?
How cold?
He seemed a little hesitant to go into it but what he told us put everything into perspective.

"Done in the right weather its reasonably safe to climb but what has killed so many is money."

I was gobsmacked when he told me that back then, it cost about $40,000 to go on an expedition and it would take two months to get to base camp or the danger zone and if the weather turns bad, well that's it, it's a no go.
But no, people think they can buy their way up... they can't.
He told me,

"My best friend died because of some impatient fool with money so after that I called it quits and said my goodbyes to Sagarmatha."

There's something primeval in making and then sitting around a fire chatting away.
Everyone has their own favourite story to tell, and we all love a good story.

We were a mix of people from all over the world and by listening to their stories, you get a good idea of their culture and upbringing, and although their experiences might be different to mine, our stories seemed quite similar.

Sat there by the fire under a blanket of stars in an infinite universe, I could feel that Curtis wanted to tell his eerie story about his Grandad's prophetic warning from the grave, but I was worried that he might be giving away a bit too much information as to why were really here,
so I jumped in with the Amazon A Go-Go frog tale...
it did not go down well.

It had been an amazing and physically demanding day and after a few beers, we just lay back on the sand staring up into the heavens and feeling the majesty of these incredible mountains. You just realise how small and insignificant you are in the universe and it really puts you in your place.

There was zero light pollution, I'd never seen a sky like it. The Milky Way in full bloom and countless shooting stars scratching the night sky. I just lay there in awe trying my best to understand the universe and all the while doing my best to ignore the real job at hand.
We had decided before we set off to never bring 'it' up and to just fully embrace this once-in-a-lifetime experience.

The next day, we were all completely rejuvenated and all up for the challenges that the day would bring.

We blasted through some amazing rapids and felt the true power of the river; the energy between us all was electric. In-between the rapids, there were calm waters where you would just cruise along the river and you could take in your surroundings.
I noticed little mounds of stones along the riverbank, obviously man-made and asked Thai what they were?

He told me that the river was regarded as one of the holiest of rivers and that the locals would put the bodies of their dead relatives on the stones and cremate their remains.
The remains would then be thrown into the river where they would be swept down the Kali Gandaki and into the Ganges which is also a sacred river.

You would see the odd tribal villager knocking about, and they were always carrying something that looked bloody heavy; they didn't waste a journey, that's for sure.
We passed under many long, thin, dodgy looking rope bridges that looked like they could snap at any minute and most certainly wouldn't take my weight.

We had a good team talk and we were all confident and buzzing, ready to take on the white water of Little Brother, a class IV rapid. Then the climax would be Big Brother, a class V, which is one grade off impossible.

Squeaky bum time.

The bond had been forged and we were a tight unit.
We would follow every instruction from Thai - our captain - who steered from the back.

The adrenaline was pumping as we took on Little Brother. One of the guys in the kayak would go out on a reconnaissance run to gauge the flow of the rapids and he would come back and tell Thai who then formed a plan of attack and give us instructions on how we would tackle it.

We set out to meet the brothers with a steely determination. The Gandaki unleashed its fury and we were at its mercy. We were just tossed and thrown around and whatever we did seemed to make no difference. It was the river that controlled us, but Thai had warned us of this and told us not to panic. He and his team knew the rapids like the back of their hands and would steer us down the path of least resistance.

If we went in, and it was very likely that at least one of us would, we had to just place our trust in the two spotters in the kayaks and the training that we had been given.
There ye go, easy.

Martin was the first to go in and within less than a minute, they got him back in the raft.
He just sat there all pissed wet through and breathless with a big smile on his face.
I'm pretty sure God got the credit for that one.
We were getting thrown about like rag dolls, everything was so fast and violent then BANG.
We hit a rock and three of us were just catapulted into the raging torrent.

WOW.

The hit from the icy-cold water just snatched the breath from me. We were taught that if you fall into the big rapids and you lose your breath, either from the shock from the cold or swallowing water, you had to turn yourself around and let the force of the water go over the back of your head enabling you to breathe and get your wits about you.
Then you would turn back around so that you could see what's coming, i.e. rocks etc., but I made a big mistake and one I'll never do again when putting a life jacket on.

I didn't tighten it up enough and bloody 'ell, did it make a difference.

When you do it correctly, the lifejacket keeps your body high up and therefore your head away from the waves.
I made the simple mistake of not tightening the jacket properly which meant that when I went into the river, my body slipped

down deeper into the water and so my face was closer to the torrent.

Just that couple of inches lower in the water meant the waves would smash you in the face. Before I could turn around to get my breath back, I took a big wave right in the chops making me choke and splutter and left me gasping for air.

I couldn't breathe.

I was completely disorientated, I didn't know forward from back, up from down or arse from elbow.

Then suddenly there was a huge WHACK to my back.

I hit a rock and any remaining air that I had left in my body was gone. Half-drowned and now winded, I was being tossed about like a pair of dirty scruds in a washing machine.

I suddenly saw the attraction to Martin's God.

The procedure was to hold your hand up to show that you were having difficulties.

I knew I was in serious trouble and was trying desperately to get a gulp of air.

I could see the other two getting back on the raft and knew that if I didn't get onto that raft pronto, I was a goner.

It felt like I was in the water for ages and by the time the kayak got to me, I was close to blacking out.

It took every last bit of energy that I had left just to hold on to the back of the kayak as he powered his way through the current and back to safety.

Curtis was laughing his bollocks off as they pulled my limp body back on board.

I lay there like a fish out of water desperately trying to gulp in the air whilst the rest of the team soldiered on through the rapids.

Even after we got through it all to the point where the river became calm and we were all high fiving each other with our paddles, I was absolutely shitting it at the thought of going back into the even more extreme rapids of the legendary Big Brother.
I told Curtis of my fears and he just said,

"tighten yer jacket up; the next rapid is only a level III, so we'll jump in together to get rid of your fears, if you fall off a horse, you just get right back on it."

I thought about the whole madness of this trip and the risk I was taking smuggling the drugs and compared it to the risk of carrying on with this boat ride.

Gimme that fucking horse.

On the next section, we didn't wait to be bounced off the boat, we just jumped into the rapids shouting,
"VALHALLA."

Curtis was bang on; now that my lifejacket was on properly, I was so much higher in the water and I could face the oncoming rocks and waves.

My confidence was back. Bring on Big Brother.

So, if this was to be my last week of freedom, then what a beautiful part of the world to spend it in.
Nepal was both exhilarating and awe inspiring, but now the reality that I had suppressed to the back of mind was here, and an even greater challenge lay ahead.

And Tonight Mathew I'm going to be ... A drug Mule

When we got back to our hotel, reality was waiting for us. Abbie had been busy and the suitcases just sat there like the eggs from the movie Alien.
It was scary just looking at them.

We picked them up one by one to feel how much heavier a case would be that had cannabis hidden in them and there didn't seem to be that much difference to a normal one, we were impressed.
We felt the lining on the cases trying to guess where it could be hidden and started sniffing all around the cases like bloodhounds for any whiff of cannabis.
I would catch myself just staring at the cases in almost a kind of disbelief that they were actually there and that we were really going to do this.

This reality had been pushed firmly to the back of our minds and we refused to acknowledge it but here we were, and to be honest, on seeing the cases and giving them a good examination, it bolstered our resolve and we felt confident that we could pull this off.

I had previously told Abbie that if there was the slightest sign of the bags or anything not looking right then it was a no-go, but there was never any pressure from anyone to do it.

Abbie knew what he was doing and who to send; those that get caught smuggling usually looked really nervous and had 'guilty as fuck' written all over them or they just got pissed and instantly attracted attention to themselves and would over-egg their performance, but Abbie was happy with us from the start.

I even got myself a disguise.

Now before you start laughing it was a very subtle but effective affair.

So, I look like your classic British yob. A well-built skinhead but as we said before, I don't have any tattoos or anything, so I just put on some nice clothes and some 'John Lennon glasses` and you wouldn't believe the difference.

I was right off the radar.

It's always the little things that make the difference.

Remember Ben Kingsley who played Ghandi?

He had those little wire glasses on and there he was, the civil rights champion who helped India to gain independence from the English through non-violent actions.

Buuut... he took those glasses off in Sexy Beast and became Don Logan the London gangster nutjob and he was equally brilliant and convincing.

So, here we go, off to the airport. Abbie had a quick word with us before we left the hotel and asked one of us to take a passport which I presumed was stolen for $500.

It was hidden in the hardback sleeve of a diary and expertly done. We agreed to that, but I point blank refused his other little extra.

He wanted me to take a small 'sample' of the resin which was wrapped in cellophane and put it under my bollocks.
I told him not a chance as anything could happen and why increase the odds of being caught just for a small sample? Curtis agreed though and I was not happy.

The way I saw it was that if Curtis got caught, then we both get caught and I wasn't having it.
Curtis came up with a compromise.

"Don't worry it's not going under my bollocks it's going **up** somewhere else."

"OK," I replied, "but you shove it up there on your own."

The departure

As soon we got there, the mood felt so different from when we first landed. It was just as full and chaotic but the atmosphere was far more tense.

There was a strong military presence, something had happened, (later I found out it was Maoist rebels) and they were on the lookout for something a lot more serious than drugs.
This kind of put my mind at ease because smuggling weapons or explosives is a lot different to smuggling cannabis and therefore they will be looking for different clues and a different kind of people, but then again, it was a similar situation to Billy Hayes from Midnight Express and they busted him.

I didn't just have the diving and golfing adventure as a story, I had made this who I was, so I was completely cloaked in my alter ego.

The first time your bags go through an X-ray machine that's designed to find hidden things and you have something hidden is quite an experience I can tell you.

There are some things that are impossible to describe and this is one.

I kind of wish that somehow you could feel the emotion and tension of what it's like just so that you could relate to what I was feeling but of course, I hope you never do.

We also had the 500 grammes hidden in the lining of the computer bag that was used as a carry-on.

I told Abbie that I didn't want a computer to put into the bag because I am completely computer illiterate and was worried that for some reason, they'd want me to switch it on or something and then I would have been well-sussed.

I always use these bags anyway because they are really handy for putting CDs, pens, books, and all other kinds of stuff in, plus my itinerary for all of my diving trips etc was in there so I was perfectly at ease with that.

We were both body searched countless times, even at the stairs that go up to the plane and then, just as I was about to go through the door onto the plane, I was searched one last time, and this guy checked all around my bollocks.

He gave me a proper feel up.

Thank fuck I didn't take the 'sample'.

Well played me.

I finally got to sit down and heard the door close.

I slowly exhaled and checked myself for any sign of an overreaction. Of course, the plane had to wait for what seemed like forever to even start moving.

Even then, as it was manoeuvring to get ready for take-off, I remembered that bit in the films where they think they have got away with it and then the plane just suddenly stops and on come the police.

The noise of the engine increased from a slow whine to a thunderous roar and we sped down the runway and finally up... up... and away.

I thanked Martin's God one more time.

There ain't half been some clever bastards

Let the madness begin!
OK, this next bit is just mental.

Nothing really makes sense and it kinda goes against all logic but I was in a whole world of madness.
Basically had to take the best, least mental option in order to get the drugs to Japan without looking suspicious.

If we turned up in Japan with a Nepalese stamp in our passports, this would get red flags flying all over the show. The Nepal run into Japan was notorious and we would almost certainly get scrutinised at customs, so we had to get the Nepal stamp removed and a Maldives stamp put in to authenticate our most splendid diving holiday.

So. Don Muang airport in Bangkok.
It's not particularly difficult to smuggle drugs through, but if you get caught, you are well and truly fucked.
I'd read about this place in many a book and seen all the stories in the newspapers of desperate foreigners getting busted and they end up looking at the death sentence or 100 years in disgusting, jam-packed conditions… if you was lucky.
So here I was with my mate carrying altogether eight kilos of drugs… **eight kilos!**

I'm sitting here, shaking my head as I'm writing this at how I tried to justify it.

My thinking was that because Thailand wasn't the destination for the drugs, and because we weren't selling the drugs there, then it wouldn't be as bad if we got caught.

Yeah, I know, as if they would give us a lighter sentence because they believed us when we said we weren't going to sell it in Thailand.
I did have experience though with this airport in my cigarette smuggling days and was wise to the fact that foreigners didn't tend to get stopped.
The only time that I knew of that a foreigner got stopped was one of my mate's brothers and that was because he took his Thai bird with him and they busted him.
He had to pay an $8,000 fine for smuggling cigarettes.

"Well... she wanted to come with me on holiday."

What a fucking knob.

Anyhow, I convinced myself well enough that this was the best option and we breezed through.
See?
Just because it's mental doesn't mean it won't work.

We stayed for a week in Thailand and went to Chinatown to get the passports sorted.
Chinatown in Thailand at night really gives me that 'Blade Runner' vibe, and even more so now with our secret mission.

I can't go into detail about how the system works for getting the passports fixed for obvious reasons, so all I can say is that we had to get them to 'The Chinaman' who would 'correct' them.

This guy really was the business though; in all the time I was involved in all of these shenanigans, none of his work was ever detected.

Of course, the rumours were rife about this mysterious craftsman and tales were told of him working both sides from Mossad and the CIA to some very extreme groups but that's the thing, when you're that good, no-one ever knows the real story and they most certainly don't go on TV or write books about it.

Like this silly twat typing away for example.

Reality removed and our fiction in place, we made plans for our next adventure.

Next stop Taiwan.

Taiwan.
Working for the CID.

By now, this was our third time running the gauntlet through airports and this time it was a walkthrough.
We didn't see one customs officer.

I bought some new aftershave and a sleeve of cigarettes and I only left the flipping bag with them in on the trolley.
I didn't realise until 20 minutes down the road in the taxi.
Oh well, considering what I was carrying, I wasn't going back for it, I can tell you that.

Keelung is the port where you catch the ferry to Okinawa and is only 40 minutes from Taipei.

Now, the first real spanner in the works was completely out of our hands and was all down to Mother Nature.

(Bloody women.)
A sodding Typhoon was on the way and all ferry crossings were off until... well, no one knew.
We originally planned for a week on 'holiday' to tick all the tourist boxes but now, that wasn't looking too good.

After almost two weeks of just hanging around and waiting for the weather to break, we got the all-clear and were eager to get it over with.

In the two weeks that we spent on holiday, we only met one person who could speak English and that was in Taipei so, on the shuttle from the ticket office to the ferry and because there was hardly anyone else on the bus, Curtis felt it was safe to talk about our little trip.
Still cautious he whispered,
"I'm a little worried about the anti-dog smell wearing off."
The cases were sprayed with a chemical that would stop the dogs from smelling what was in them.
We had two fucking weeks to talk about this and he brings it up now.
I was not happy.
I took a little look around the bus and to my horror, I saw another westerner sat a few seats back on the opposite side. I figured that this guy could speak English and quickly gave Curtis a nudge with my knee complete with a 'zip it' sign with my hand. It was a bit of a surprise to see another westerner but there was no chance he'd overheard Curtis.

"Hello mate, wow, another white man." I laughed nervously.
The guy replied.
"Oh hi, I'm Jim. You on the ferry to Okinawa?"
Something didn't seem right with this guy and straight away I thought, *FUCKING COPPER.*
I mean, he knew damn well we were going on the ferry to Okinawa because this is the frigging shuttle to the ferry.
Also, no one says 'Hi, I'm Jim'.
Why introduce yourself like that?
It felt odd that there was only us and three other people who looked like they were Taiwanese in the whole bloody port.
"You travelling, pal?" I asked.
"No, I live here teaching English. I'm just off to do my visa run. It's a real pain in the arse but it's gotta be done."

Hmm, I felt a little better about his response.
This wasn't just a little ferry crossing of a couple of hours or so, it was a 20-hour overnight marathon of a trip in typhoon weather conditions.

When we bought the tickets, we were told it was a VIP style extravaganza.
Six floors, cocktail lounge, theatre, ballroom, indoor and outdoor pools, 5-star restaurants, a nightclub, and what I was really looking forward to , virtual golf.
Wow this was some new, high-tech shit.

Good news, bad news.

The good news was that the typhoon missed us, and having had a few bad crossings in stormy weather before to France and Ireland, I was more than relieved to be having what should be a very smooth crossing.

The bad news was that - I guess - because of the weather warnings, no one else wanted to go on the ferry, so there was just me, Curtis, Jim, and the other three from the mini-bus on the whole ship.
Because so few tickets had been sold, everything, and I do mean everything, else was closed.

All we had was one vending machine, but it had everything that we needed.
Beer, cigarettes, pot noodles, and coffee for the morning.
What more could a man want?
I'll tell you what... virtual bloody golf and all that other VIP-style bollocks.

God knows how many rooms there were, but we finally found ours and when we opened the door, guess who was sat there?

"Hi guys."

It was fucking Jim!

"Oh there must be a mix-up, they must think we're together."

"Hmm, yeah," I replied. "OK…I'll go and sort it out."

Was this a setup for him to get some info?

'Of course not Ste, get ye shit together', I told myself, as I was trying to find a member of staff on a flipping ghost ship.

I finally got it sorted, and as soon as the doors closed to our now, private room Curtis said,

"That's a pig."

"Oh, piss off." I spat back at him. "I was hoping it was just me freaking out and you were going to say stop being so paranoid."

He carried on,

"It's his hairdo, they can't hide it. They have a smell like an office or something. Oh…fuckin' 'ell."

He had that unmistakeable look of someone shitting their pants on his face.

I knew damn well what he meant.

I mean why?

How?

Is it just a certain type that wants to be a police officer?

Curtis was on one:

"Why would they put us in room together when the ship is bloody empty for fucks sake?"

"Curtis, calm down and think about it. It's a simple mistake."

I was trying to convince him and myself.

"We did look like were travelling together when we boarded and think about it, why put a copper right on our tail like this, it's too obvious, what would be the point? We're here now and there's no turning back so let's chill and have a beer or ten."

I felt a lot better after saying this.
I'd convinced both of us that we were just being paranoid and jumping to conclusions.
Jim or Sid (CID, get it?) as I now called him in my head came and sat with us.

Another round of said, not said.
"Can I sit and have a beer with you lads?"

"Of course you can pal, sit theesel down and cut thee sel a butt as my old mate's Grandad Bill used to say haha."
AAAAGHHHHHH. HE'S A FUCKING COPPER! HE'S ON TO US, THROW THE BAGS OVER THE SIDE.

"It's really quiet on the boat, isn't it? We've got it all to ourselves."

"Yeah, must have been the typhoon putting everyone off."
FUCK OFF! FUCK OFF! FUCK OFF! FUCK OFF!

Curtis wasn't a big drinker so went to bed early, leaving me and Sid to empty the vending machine of beer while continuing our cosy little chat.

I don't know if it was the alcohol or just the fact that the more we talked about this and that, the more I felt at ease.

Sid had been living in Taiwan for a few years now, was settled down, married, and had a young un on the way.

He'd previously been traveling around Southeast Asia, where he met and fell love with a Taiwanese woman. He proudly showed off her photo in his wallet.

"Very pretty, I must say, mate," I said, "good catch."

" Yeah, I fell in love, and it put an end to my backpacking journey and... " He had a little jokey look around.
"I had to smuggle drugs to stay."

(after a slight pause) ... "Really?"
AAAAAAAGHHHHHHHHHH... I FUCKING KNEW YOU WERE A COPPER. THE BASTARD FILTH. A PIG. A PEELER. BOBBIE THE BASTARD PLOD. AAAAAAAAAAAAAAGHH, WE'RE FUCKED.

Internally I collapsed, externally I think I got away with it.

"Wow. Where to? Japan?"
You're trying to reel me in, get info out of me from a cheeky confession like we're all mates, aren't you?

"Oh no, it's far too dangerous there. The Japanese customs would be all over it."

"Really? I've never even thought about that, but yeah, I guess they would. They're quite high tech, the Japs. Yeah, they'll be on the ball."
You really think I'm gonna give you any kind of a clue that I know anything about Japanese customs?

"Jeeeesus, you must have been nuts. What did you smuggle?"

OK, let's play the game... I'll be the tourist and you be the smuggler. It's your move.

"Oh, it was just a bit of hash. One kilo at the bottom on my rucksack haha."

"Haha, sod that. Ye must have been mad."

You keep trying pal. You think that I'm going to slip up after a few beers?

"I was young and in love I guess, haha, oh yes… the things you do, eh?"

I felt sick to my stomach and my mouth was drying up. All I wanted to do was get away from him and warn Curtis, but I knew I had to play it cool.

We had been chatting for about ten minutes and I felt that was an acceptable amount of time to look comfortable in front of Sid but also, I would be able to retreat to the cabin and unleash my agony onto Curtis without arousing suspicion.

You have to understand how difficult it is to not look or act guilty when you are guilty.
You suddenly become over analytical about everything that you do.
I mean who thinks that chatting for ten minutes is an acceptable amount of time? No one, but when you're bloody guilty you do.
The ironic thing is that in trying to not look guilty you actually end up looking fucking guilty.

I got back to our cabin.

"Mate, wake up... Curtis, wake up... he's DEA."

"Eh? What?"

"Sid just told me how he used to smuggle hash to Taiwan!"

I told Curtis of the conversation that I had with him word for word, and we went through it a couple of times to look for clues.
Well, it could be just a crazy coincidence that the **one** time I'm smuggling cannabis is the **one** time a random guy tells me about the **one** time he smuggled cannabis.

"Right, let's throw the bags off the back," said Curtis.

With Curtis now joining me in complete panic mode, that made me go in to, 'OK, OK, let's just stop and think' mode.

"What would he have to gain by telling me that? If he was the plod then he wouldn't be alone, would he? So, if they're onto us, we will be being watched. Just in case we do throw the bags over... yeah?"

We went over every scenario, good and bad until the early hours and decided to keep the cases.

I told Curtis,

"Mate, let's just get some sleep and hope for the best, eh?"

I watched some international news channel to take my mind off things and saw they had put a picture up of John Peel.

I thought, *Oh, this won't be good.*

John Peel, 25th October 2004. RIP.

Oh bugger.

I liked John Peel and used his death to put everything into some kind of context.

"Ya see, it could be worse."

Red sky at morning...

I woke up just before sunrise. I'd had a terrible night's sleep so jumped in the shower to clear my head but I couldn't stop thinking about what Jim had said the night before.
I was going around in circles thinking:
What if?
Is he?
Should I?
I had a word with myself:
'Stop bloody over thinking it! Just stick to the plan.
I'm a normal everyday tourist doing normal everyday touristy things.
I'm not a bellend smuggling drugs!'

I made a strong black coffee and went for a walk, just wandering along the bottom deck and ended up at the front rail Titanic-style but with no fit bird. Just a brew and a fag.

The cloudless sky was getting brighter announcing the imminent arrival of the sun. There was an eerie yet calming sound of the bow cutting through the flat sea accompanied by the low hum from the engine.
I took a deep breath, filling my lungs with the serenity.
I was completely alone but could hear the faint cries of seagulls, we must be getting near to land.

I glossed through my whole life, pondering on how the hell I've ended up here, on this insane journey.

This has to be the most stupid thing I've ever done.

As I was coming to terms with my looming fate, I bore witness to the cultural reference 'Land of the rising sun'. The reddest sun I have ever seen was slowly rising between two islands.

It was like a picture postcard.

It was absolutely stunning.

For those 10 blissful minutes I didn't have a care in the world.

Back in the cabin Curtis was now up and about.
"Reyt pal, let's not go over that again and get back on track as to what we're doing here, yeah?"
Curtis took my cue and we both dropped into character.
If you play the part for long enough, then you'll become it (That was my logic anyway).
"Let's hope the waters will have cleared for a good dive, hopefully the day after, eh? Said Curtis.
"Well, it is what it is," I replied.
"The forecast isn't that bad but at the least we'll get some good golf in, I can't wait. I've always wanted to hit the fairways in Naha."
We both look at each other.
Curtis nods.
I put my fake spectacles on and nod back…
"Reyt, lets crack on."

We disembark at Okinawa and Jim is already ahead of us.
"Morning pal, how's the hangover?" I asked.
"I've felt better," he replied.

I could be wrong, but I feel he regrets telling me about his 'little run'.
Alcohol really does set the voice free.

We we're told from Abbie that going to Okinawa was a cheeky little bypass, and although it was a pain in the arse to go such a long way around, patience would pay off as smugglers rarely use this route. Armed with this knowledge Abbie had used this alternative previously and knew that there would only be one or two customs officers there.

Customs at Okinawa was understaffed so they weren't too rigorous with the inspections. I mean, that's why we went from Thailand to Nepal, Nepal to Tibet, white water rafting, near death experience, Nepal to Thailand for passport exchange, Thailand to Taiwan, Taiwan to Okinawa, 20-hour Ghost trip, undercover copper followed by near shit pants experience.

All this to get a quick walk through at customs in Okinawa.
We walk down the gangway off the ferry and...

The best laid plans...
Ten fucking custom officers waiting for us.
Suddenly the gangway felt more like a gangplank.
Was I right all along?
Had Jim signalled ahead and arranged a greeting party for us?
Whatever, stay in character and just play the part.
The feeling that we had been busted actually gave me a calming effect.
Nothing to lose so just see it through.

The Taiwanese passengers just breezed through, a quick check of the passports and off they went.
Jim only had a small carry on and waltzed through saying,

"ok guys I'll see you tonight."
I swear he looked at an officer and nodded. *Yep, them two*!

We were both led to separate big metal tables with five Customs officers each.
I got the boss - captain? - I don't know, but he had my passport and was asking all sorts of questions while the other four were going through everything, feeling the lining of **all** the cases, then off to an x-ray machine at the side.

Whilst inspecting my passport the customs officer asked,

"Mr. Beattie how are you today?"

I replied,

" kon ish ee wa... haha, sorry your English is a lot better than my Japanese but I'm trying", pointing to my Basic how to speak Japanese handbook.

"Ahh velly goord. How rong you stay sir?"
His English wasn't the best, to be brutally honest, but I wasn't going to tell him, was I?

"Well, we planned to stay for two weeks but will have to see how it goes now because this typhoon has ruined our plans of diving around the small islands but, not to worry."

"Oh, you go see war museums?"

"To be honest, nah, not my kind of thing, I'm more for the Karaoke"

As he was rooting through my stuff in the computer case, I pointed to the condoms and said,

"hey, I might get lucky."
We both laughed in acknowledgment of my meaning.
I was very aware of not babbling on, which is a total give away that you're nervous and overcompensating.

In poker, it's a dead giveaway that someone is trying to look confident whilst quite obviously bluffing.

I was just casually looking around when I saw a sign on the wall.
NO DRUGS. NO GUNS.
NO PORNOGRAPHIC MATERIALS.

I had a stash of cheap DVDs that I'd bought in Taiwan. There was a few blueys (erotic movies) mixed in with them and as he went through them, I said,

"oops," pointing up to the sign. "I didn't realise, sorry," giving him a cheeky little look, knowing full well they wouldn't be too bothered.

"Ah, no problem. Haha."

I couldn't believe how well I was doing, and my confidence was rising.
I casually looked over to the officers checking the cases and I could see that this was more of a lesson than them actually scrutinising the cases.
The extra staff were trainees rather than special ops brought in by Jim the bastard to smash this international drug ring.

I thought to myself, *'we're gonna do this, we're gonna fucking do this.'*

I looked over to Curtis who was getting the same treatment as me. He looked back at me and his eyes widened, and I could just tell he was thinking the same.

'We're gonna fucking do it.'

His secret weapon and one of the reasons I wanted to go with him is that you really would think that butter wouldn't melt in his mouth and it was working like a charm.
This must have been some kind of training day for the younger staff and with the ferries all being off for over a week, they seized this opportunity for a good old practice.

Finally.
Thankfully, I heard:

"OK, Mr. Beattie, enjoy your stay."

And off we went to a taxi just outside.
My mouth was a dry as Gandhi's flip flop.
The only thing left that could go wrong was the Colombo moment...

'Just one more thing...'

We got in the back of the taxi still in character and started talking about how the ferry crossing wasn't that bad while secretly we gave each other the slightest of fist pumps...

We did it!

We bloody well did it!!!

The Road to Tokyo

It wasn't until we got into our hotel room, double-checked the door to make sure it was locked, and took one last look through the spyhole, did we give each other a big hug and start laughing.

"CID Jim! Haha, ye soft twat," I said with great relief.

"I could have sworn he gave customs the nod," Curtis replied.
He thought for a minute then continued,
"what if they've let us through to follow us to the drop-off?"

"Right, pack it in. We did it mate, we fucking well did it." We laughed again. Of course we'd done it.

I went back to my own room and, as seen on Banged Up Abroad (a cracking job of that reenactment btw), and fell back on the bed almost in tears, overwhelmed with emotions.
I'd say mostly relief, combined with the comedown from the adrenaline that was earlier coursing through my veins.
I wasn't happy or elated and these weren't feelings of joy.
Not one thought of, *'Yes, I'm loaded'*.
Nope, just pure relief that I hadn't been caught.
The thought of what had happened just 15 minutes earlier was still running riot in my mind.

How the hell did we both so calmly weather the storm at customs?

Phew.

    We had a fun night in Naha, the capital of Okinawa. We ate some great new foods, did some karaoke, of course, and found this cool little jazz bar.
    It was fairly empty, so I took this opportunity and asked the band if I could play and they were sound.
I got up and jammed with them on the drums and we played a cross metal/jazz mix of Metallica's One.
They were absolutely amazing musicians.
    Then, after the band had finished, a Japanese guy that had been watching came up to the stage and in that really apologetic, constantly bowing, stereotypical Japanese way, asked if he could play a song that he had written.
Well, as I'd turned the gig into a bit of a jam night, then of course he could.
    He strapped on a guitar and played what only can be described as the best, worst song I'd ever heard.
It was like a crap Oasis-type tune, with just a couple of very predictable chords and sung in Japanese.
You could tell he hadn't performed it to anyone, let alone in public, so we all encouraged him by clapping along to the rhythm.
He sang with such emotion that by the end, he was bawling his eyes out.
God only knows what that bitch had done to the poor fella but.

    If only she could see him now. Then maybe, just maybe, she'd take him back.'

    (That's what I got from his heartfelt performance anyway).

FUCK THAT, KAITO, SHE'S NOT WORTH IT.

I gave him a big manly hug and by this time, I was skriking too. Mostly from the beer and Kaito's performance, but also the pent-up relief from getting away with smuggling a shitload of drugs decided to get in on this emotional outpouring.
I looked over at Curtis and he was crying too.

"Ya soft twat, look at you." I bawled.

"Fucking look at you, ya tart," he replied.

And with that we just carried on drinking, crying and singing.

"KANPAI."

We spent a couple of days in Naha then we were off on the ferry again. A nice, drama-free 25-hours to Kagoshima on mainland Japan.

Once again, I was able to bear witness to the most incredible sunrise, but this time it was under very different circumstances.
This time, I didn't have the dark clouds of impending doom hanging over me, just clear skies and the one small hurdle that involves a quick bag exchange with the Yakuza.
Japan's biggest mafia outfit in Japan's biggest city...

Piece o' piss!

We caught the bullet train to Tokyo; this was our first experience of high-tech Japan and it was amazing.
It really felt futuristic.

Our trip took us through Hiroshima, and although there were no physical signs to be seen of the atomic bomb being dropped, it still left me with an eerie feeling just knowing what had happened.
Another one to stick into the 'context' bank the next time I'm ever in a pickle.

Now, remember when I said earlier it was a nice drama-free trip?
Yeah, well for me it was but, on the train, Curtis had a different experience.

I was fast asleep, lost in a stress-free world, when suddenly Curtis burst in.

"Oh Jesus Christ, I nearly jumped off the flipping train."

Ah, reality...

"Eh? What you on about? And calm down for fuck's sake,"

"So, that last stop? As we pulled into the station, there was a shitload of police waiting for the train and as it stopped, they were all running up and down looking through all the windows and it looked like they pointed at me and then they all jumped on."

"Fuck me… go on."

"I just froze. I didn't know what to do. They all came bounding down the carriage and I was thinking, *'OH SHIT, THIS IS IT'*. I thought they had guns and everything and I was about to put my hands up."

He was almost breathless by this point and paused to catch his breath.
I was just laid there, eyes wide, beckoning him on.

"And?"

"Well... they just went past me and buggered off down the train. I've no idea who they were after."

With a feeling of relief **and** despair I groaned and looked down into my lap.
It was at this moment when I realised that I had been asleep, laid back in the reclining chair,
legs spread,
with a raging hard on for all the train to see.

Imagine being arrested with a lob on.

I just looked at him and sighed.

Bloody drama queen.

The End Game

I couldn't wait to get shut of these bloody bags and what was in them.
Just one last hurdle before the finishing line but we had no idea who was doing the pickup.
I was expecting a couple of Yakuza heavies to do the pick-up. All tattooed up and looking mean as fuck.
I was kinda intrigued to meet them. It's not every day you meet the real deal.

We had a plan of leaving the stash in one room and the meet and exchange to be made in another.
One thing was for sure, no one was getting anything until we got the money.

Now in the highfalutin drug world, I guess $18,000 isn't that much money, but to us, it was enough to get done in over. It seems a bit silly looking back, but we were of the mindset that it's better to be safe than sorry and I'm not about to have my arse handed to me over 18 grand.

So, we just sat back and chilled, having a few bottles of Asahi beers waiting for our pay day.
Nothing to worry about, it's almost over.
Knock, Knock, Knock.
I looked through the spy hole and see a reyt shifty-looking Middle Eastern lad, constantly looking up and down the corridors.

I opened the door with the chain lock on.

"Yes?"

"Abbie send."

"OK, cool."

I unlocked the door and let him in.

"You want a beer, buddy?"

"NO. BAGS."

He started looking around.

"WHERE BAGS?"

Well, that's the mutual bullshit out of the way.

"Money first, he counts," I said pointing to Curtis. "Then I go get the bags... OK?"
At this point it got pretty uneasy and he just says,
"GET THE FUCKING BAGS, ME SPEAK NO ENGLISH."
Although the weather was a nice 20 degrees, this fucker was sweating his bollocks off.

"Hey, no need to swear, ring Abbie now."

He was starting to piss me off.

"Ste, I don't feel too good about this guy."

"Me neither, mate."

He was on the phone to someone then said,
"I go, I go."

We were more than happy to see the back of this one.
I went and got a trusty seven iron from the golf bag to help with the communication problems.

We heard nothing for an hour; we tried calling Abbie but nothing and then, again…
KNOCK, KNOCK, KNOCK.
Now it could have just been our imagination but it seemed a lot louder, a more aggressive knock.
I looked through the spy hole again to see the same guy but he wasn't alone. Had he brought back up?

"Curtis, take a look, there's two of them now"

My heart was pumping big time.
Curtis took one look and said,
"Oh thank fuck. It's Kavos from two years ago."
Oh, the relief… again.

"Kavos, this is Ste."

He was such a nice cool guy and straight away, I was at ease.

"Kavos, what's the crack with this guy?"

"Oh, he works for me in my restaurant. It's his first time so his pants were shitting. He said the bald guy, (Kavos nodded to me) **you**, looked like you were going to attack him."

"He's not wrong, I fucking was. My pants were shitting too."

We all laughed and for us it was mostly out of relief because finally…
Thankfully…
Fanfuckingtastically…
It really was over.

We got paid, spent a few days Billy-big-timing it in Roppongi and then back…

Back to what I was now calling home...

Thailand.

Tsunami

What a great buzz to get back to Thailand.
Me and the Silverback went on holiday for a couple of weeks to Koh Samui and Phuket at the beginning of December. Then it was a quick trip back home to the UK to see friends and family and then fly back to Thailand for Christmas day.

On Boxing Day morning, I was still recovering from the long flight, but red wine and Yeti love was the main culprit. I'd started to get phone calls which I ignored as usual, but there were a lot more than usual, so I knew something was up. It was Woz.

"Ey up, you OK?"

"Eh… yeah, just a bit knackered. Why?"

I was confused as I'd only just seen him a few days before.

"There's been a massive earthquake and a tidal wave has hit Thailand, it's all over the news. They're saying loads have died."

"Oh shit, we've not felt anything, but we were up all-night drinking, partying, and the rest."

Thankfully it was the opposite side of Thailand, so Pattaya was safe.
We were lucky the Tsunami didn't hit the week before when we stopped at Koh Phi Phi for five days.
I later changed it to Koh poo poo; this was after Wanna found out that I was going on a diving trip.

What happened was that I wanted to go on a diving trip but it was really early in the morning and I knew that she wouldn't go because she's proper lazy, but I asked her anyway and she wasn't interested.
I booked it and found out that I was sharing the trip with five Russian models.
I always used to wind her up saying Russian girls are better looking than Thai girls so when I told her that I was sharing the boat, she soon changed her tune, giving it,

'Oh I'll come'.

I told her she couldn't because it was too late and I'd already booked. She wasn't happy and then she did something really weird.
She started praying to Buddha. I was like,

"Oh my God, you're mental."

But there she was, on her knees praying to a fat bald bloke. (That's usually me… WAHAY).
Anyway, all this to stop me from not going.
You'll not believe what happened and to be honest,
neither do I.

I GOT THE SHITS.

I'm not lying, cross my heart hope to die, yada yada, but the next day I had arse gravy for the next five days.
I was pretty much just rooted to the toilet and couldn't go on the trip.

Do I believe her prayers worked?
Do I shite.
Is the fickle finger of fate a complete bastard at times?
Yes, it is.
Does Wanna believe she has a direct line to Buddha?
I'm sure she does.

Once again though, we have to put things into context, especially religion, fate, and fortune.
We were lucky to be on the other side of Thailand when the Tsunami struck the poor souls who we'd been with only the week before.
Koh Phi Phi was where The Beach was filmed and is a popular tourist area and because the island is barely above sea level, it never stood a chance.
On the TV, we saw the distinctive green roofs of the bungalows where we had stayed only one week earlier being washed away.

Such good people and a sad loss... RIP.

Never, again.

When I was laid there on the bed in Okinawa after we'd got through customs, I swore to myself that I'd never do that again, and with 100% conviction, I meant it.

Never, never, never again.
A song by Discharge, one of my favourite punk bands, was just going round and round in my head.
The money soon ran out but thankfully, I was fine about going back to the UK to work by this stage.
I'd had my mad do and was ready to face reality.

Over the next four years, I got into the groove and back on the trowel laying bricks. Head down, arse up to save money and take the longest holiday I could afford.

I'd also started playing poker and although I never won anything major, every now and then I'd get a nice little windfall. Usually in the region of four to eight grand, and that would see me right for a good few months.

Then in 2007, I had a water-skiing accident and crushed my bloody neck. I was stiff as a board for the next week and although it eventually wore off, it came back with a vengence.

I went to the doctors and after several scans, they diagnosed that I'd trapped a nerve in my neck which affected my whole right arm. I was actually working in Perth, Australia at the time and it got so bad that I couldn't even hold a beer, never mind a bricklaying trowel.

So, it was options time again.

1. Go home to the UK, get on the dole or claim sick pay while waiting to get the nerve damage fixed. I was told that I could get an operation but even then, it was far from guaranteed to work.
2. Play poker. To play the game for a living you need a bank roll, and I simply didn't have the money to back me up.
3. Smuggle drugs.

Let's not beat about the bush, I obviously went for option number three.

In the four years since I last did my little run, no one had been caught which is bloody good going.
Many of my mates were still at it and Alex had been doing it for five years by now, for Christ's sake.

Ring ring... ring ring... ring ring.

"Abbie... it's Damage."

"Motherfucker, haha, let's get to work."

London Calling

I met Abbie in Bangkok where he took me to another side of the city that I knew nothing about.

So here I was, Mr. High Society (or Hi-So as they say in Thailand). I'd finally made it to the top, enjoying fine dining at some fancy restaurant.

The following day over breakfast, we came up with a plan that suited me.
I was to fly to Mumbai in India and create my new character which was to be a businessman buying silk and bringing samples of the finest wears back to England to be sold to some lucky lady.

Later, he took me to Bangkok's top nightclub where I was offered any of the Russian prostitutes that were lounging around the place, all at Abbie's expense of course.
The food was excellent but annoyingly, there were only small portions.
I remember thinking, "*This is not for me, this.*"

The club was too loud and full of pretentious twats just showing off and the 'ladies' on offer were more like junkies than high-class escorts.
This was such a contrast to the Thai bar girls who enjoy what they do and are fun to be around, but here, they looked like they had to be off their face just to get through the night.

As I've said earlier, prostitution in Thailand is so misunderstood but with the Russian girls, it was plain to see that they were a really sorry lot.

When I got back to London, I was to meet my market trading partner in Camden Town. Oh…and I was smuggling in four kilos of cannabis resin too.

My good mate Scotty would also be doing a little run to London via Goa, but I decided on doing the run separately. Even though Scotty looked perfect with his innocent, well-dressed everyday kind of look - I knew he'd done this many times before… far too many times - I felt he was too blasé.

He had no real cover story planned and to be honest, he really didn't give a fuck. I mean it worked for him so…

I'd always wanted to go to Goa ever since I was a kid. I remember it was a big fancy holiday destination on 'Wish You Were Here'.

So, this was ideal, I could tag the holiday onto my business trip to Mumbai. Perfect.

Goa was Portugal's first Asian territory and served as a base for four and a half centuries so there is a Portuguese influence within the food which was right up my street.
The meat was so tender and the people were super-friendly too but the beach and sea was so overrated in my eyes and bloody dangerous.

On the second day, we went for a swim, and I'd just said to Scotty,

"Ey, I can feel the current really dragging my legs back."

When suddenly, the lifeguards blew the whistle calling everyone back onto the beach.

We were only chest deep in the water but it was a real struggle fighting the current to get out.

We found out a few days later that two middle-aged British women sadly drowned that day.

Mad Scot's an Englishman

Mad Scotty as he's known, got that name for being a top, fun lad.
He was always off his trolley on something or other but never violent, just bloody mischievous.
You never saw him in a bad mood and he always had a big infectious smile on his face and would pull the birds with his cheeky banter.

We all have a chink in our armour, some worse than others, and unfortunately, Scotty's was heroin.
It was a bad problem for him back in his hometown of Wakefield in West Yorkshire and over here in Thailand, his drugs of choice were yaba and ice, but mainly beer, which did seem the better option.

Down in Goa, he bought a shit load of Diazepam and would munch on about 20 tabs per night, all washed down with a rake of beers and inevitably, by the end of the night, he would fall asleep everywhere and anywhere.
It could get quite embarrassing and I remember having to carry him off home, then the next day go searching for what he'd lost; phone, wallet, Mp3 player...

When we got back up to Mumbai, we, well not we...
I, decided to have an early night to be up early ready for the 11 a.m. flight.

Scotty?

Nah. He got in about five a.m.

So, at 8 a.m., I was up and about, getting ready for the flight and all the while banging on at Scotty to get his arse into gear telling him,

"Scotty, wake up pal, there's a brew here for ye."

Nothing.
Not one movement came from him. I even did the cold water from the fridge straight into the face...
Nope...
Nada...
Nowt.

By the time I was ready to leave, I gave him a good hard slap across the face and as that stirred him into a reaction I said,

"reyt... I'm off, ye big tit, and you need to get ye shit together or you'll miss the bloody flight, pal."

I had to wait ten minutes for the taxi to arrive and just as I was leaving the foyer, I heard,

"Oi... **OI!**"

He somehow, got up just in time; he was bloody lucky I'd packed his bag and got his clothes ready for him.
What a stinking mess he was. I decided to stop and get a coffee.

"Mate, you look a mess. Just remember, once we get to the airport, you're on your own, pal, we don't know each other. Yeah?"
As soon as we got to the taxi drop off outside of departures, I said goodbye and good luck.

I was really worried for him.
I wasn't worried that he'd get caught, I was worried that he wouldn't be allowed on the plane because he was still so drunk/doped up.
I was off, and this time it really did feel like a doddle.

I guess sorting Scotty out was a distraction and took my mind off getting through customs.
I put my big red suitcase on the conveyor belt of the X-ray machine.

Two sets of suitcases had been dropped off earlier the day before. One big one and one small one each.
The problem was that they were all the same colour and if we were travelling together, it would have stuck out like a sore thumb.
So, you can see why I was so keen not to be travelling together. Even more so now with Scotty off his tits.

So, everything was going fine until...

Bang.

A trolley hit me in the back of my legs. I turned around, and there was Scotty, sniggering like a little kid.

"Oops... sorry mate."

What the hell was he thinking?
He'd shoved his red bag right behind mine and what happened next was like a scene from Laurel & Hardy.

Somehow, as we went through the body scanner, he got to the bags first and took mine which was the first one through. Carrying on with the act that we didn't know each other, I casually said,

"oops, sorry mate, my bag was the first one through. Hey, they look the same, don't they? Haha."

"No, Damage, mine is the red one."

I spoke as quietly and as calmly as I could.

"Scotty, we both have a red fucking bag, you prick, we're not together, remember? Stop making a scene."

Off I went to check-in, absolutely fuming with him but thankfully the check-in was all fine.
Onto the next stage, immigration.
Oh boy, it was chock-a-block.
A massive queue that looked to be hundreds of people long but hey-ho, I had plenty of time.

I got chatting to an American guy who was a sales rep for some cigarette company. He was quite an interesting guy and he liked my idea of the cheap silk market and although it had obviously been done before, he thought it was still a good business idea.
So, just as I was telling him how I'd travelled alone all around Mumbai looking for the best deals, I died inside as I heard...

"Damage... DAMAGE."

We looked over to the front of the queue where Scotty was waving a passport.

"Damage, I've got your passport, pal."

I truly was gobsmacked.

"Ey up, Damage, I've got ya passport here, come and get it"

Giving me the big wink, wink.
What a fucking knob.
Ya see, in Scotty's head, he was doing me a favour because having jumped the queue himself, he then came up with the master plan of helping a mate out.
I was Johnny on the spot. I said to the Yank,

"Oh no, not this idiot again. He was in my hotel last night pissed out of his head… em, sorry, drunk not angry haha."

I waved my passport to last night's drunken stranger and shouted over the mass of people in the queue:

"Its Ok, I've got mine here, there must be some mistake, mate."

Shaking my head, I turned around and said to my new buddy,

"Just ignore him."

We eventually got through and I was off on my way to find my gate when I saw Scotty going into the toilets.
I checked there was no one about and followed him in.

"Scotty, for fuck's sake, ye utter bell end, we're supposed to be travelling alone, you're gonna blow our cover."

"Oh, give over, I've done this a billion times. I didn't have you down as a flapper, Damage."

I really wanted to twat him or at least give him a good punch in the gut thinking **that** might help him get the message, but I just shook my head and walked away saying,

"Please Scotty... please get it into your head. We're not together."

From the toilets, it was down some escalators to one more X-ray machine before our gate and boarding, and as I was watching my hand luggage go through, I went back into character, smiling at the last security officer.

'Not long now, ah… I'm almost there.'
And then….
From the top of the escalators, a loud Yorkshire voice came crashing down onto me.

"DAMAGE, 'AVE YE GOT ANY RUPEES? I NEED CHANGE FOR THE VENDING MACHINE, PAL."

I just stood there staring at him.
I didn't say a word.
I was so angry, I actually thought that it would be worth doing the 15 years or whatever just to kick his fucking head in right now. I would feel better doing the time with the satisfaction of having twatted this absolute fucking moron.
I'm not kidding you now, reader, I actually went through this thought process.
I just turned my back on him.
It was almost like, 'you've just broke me'.
I might as well just stick my underpants on my head and run around shouting,

'I'M SMUGGLING DRUGS'.

Anyway, I walked onto the plane and took my seat.
Scotty was sat away from me and fortunately, he just fell fast asleep, probably still recovering from the night before but, whatever.
He didn't bother me anymore and I just ignored him.

For years that was a catchphrase around Pattaya,

"Damage, 'ave ye got any rupees"?

Even when I told him much later on about how angry I was with him at the time, he was still oblivious as to why.

Scotty was from a lovely family, and I met them not long after. He just loved to party and get off his rocker.
There was never a dull moment with him, that's for sure.
He could be very thoughtful and sent lots of letters to me in Japan and always signed them off with,

'Damage, 'ave ye any Yen'?
Haha, he was a funny cunt.

He told me how Thailand was finished and was saving up to go and open a bar in Cambodia which was the new up and coming place. He wanted me as his bar & entertainment manager. I was well up for that.

Four years later, Scotty died under suspicious circumstances in Pattaya. RIP, brother.

There's something about Wakefield.

When I was writing the book, I got in touch with a few mates just to jog my memory. One of the lads reminded me about Simon (Pieman) who was also from Wakefield.
This is Pieman's story.

One night, Pieman got off his tits on a cocktail of drugs and came up with the fantastic idea of robbing his local post office.
So off he went to do the robbery.
Pieman was standing in the queue with his balaclava on patiently waiting his turn.
He walks up to the counter and does the classic,

"Give me all your money."

In his best, roughy toughy gangster voice.
The woman behind the counter says,

"Simon? Is that you? What are you doing? You'd better get ya 'sen home before you get into bother."

It was Sheila, she went to bingo with his mum.
Not quite knowing what to do, he leaves.
By this time, the police had been called and were on the lookout for Simon who was last seen catching the number seven bus to Wrenthorpe.

Not long after, the police arrested Simon on the bus...

He was still wearing his fucking balaclava.

Amsterdam

So, as it turns out, all that drama with Mad Scotty actually did me a lot of good, mentally.
If I was ever going to get caught, then surely it would have been the pantomime episode with Scotty at Mumbai airport.
I felt a lot more confident and at ease with doing a run now.

A few months down the line and it just became like a regular job and having to go through Europe was more of an inconvenience than anything.
The system we had was so good that everyone was getting through.

Having to catch a flight into Europe from Thailand, pick up the bags, and then a couple of days later, catch a plane back - which was a 15-hour flight - was becoming a pain in the arse to be honest.
The risk factor wasn't the same and I too, was becoming a bit blasé.

I could now relate to Mad Scotty and Smix and understood why they got drunk or whatever and really just didn't give a fuck. It was all becoming a bit boring.
It's mad I know, but you kind of miss the stress, paranoia, and the cat and mouse game that was being played out.

Meet Jake. A new friend of mine who was now also part of our band of merry men and had told me about his last trip to Amsterdam.

"It's a piece of piss, mate. I got a flight to Austria and information from 'friends' on the inside had guaranteed that on this certain time and date, there would be no customs officers to deal with at the airport. Then, just catch the train up to The Dam."
Ok, fair enough. So it was off to India to make the pickup.

India's a fascinating place, beautiful and at the same time disgusting. I just couldn't get my head around the fact that there was so much wealth and such abject poverty all on the same doorstep. India is just full of contradictions.

Dharavi in Mumbai is one of the largest slums in the world with a population of over one million, yet they can put people into space. It's just ridiculous.

The class system and the years of British rule made it what it is, and it has the best and yet the worst of human nature. I'll never understand it.

On this trip, the pickup was in the capital, New Delhi, and of course I used the trip to my full advantage to make it a holiday, whilst all the while bolstering my silk trader cover story.
I visited The Taj Mahal in Agra which is only a few hours away by an interesting train journey with all the chaos you'd expect. Are you ready for an interesting fact?

'Yes Steven', I hear you say.

The Pillars (Minarets) that surround the Taj Mahal are designed in such a way that they slightly lean outwards, and if there was an earthquake for example, the pillars would fall away from the tomb. Also, because of the slight lean outwards it creates an optical illusion that makes the pillars look perfectly vertical.
Good, eh?

That's one for the pub and my excuse for all the dodgy brick pillars I've built.
Also, the guy who designed it was imprisoned by the Emperor's youngest son who eventually became King (after imprisoning his dad) and he imprisoned the creator of the Taj Mahal in Agra fort so that he would be forced to see what he created everyday but could never touch it.
What a cunt!

   Holiday over and it was time to get to work.
   Everything went smoothly at Delhi airport but things took a turn when I landed in Vienna.
I was told that it would be a walkthrough from our 'friends' on the inside but when I arrived, there was a customs officer.
   Oh bollocks.
I knew this bag wouldn't pass a customs check; I mean that's why I chose this route.
   walkthrough my arse.
   As I was waiting for my bag to come around on the carousel, I was keeping a subtle eye on the customs fella.
I reassured myself and thought,
   Ok. The odds of me not being stopped here are fairly good so, just crack on and act normal.
Here it comes.
   'Should I let it go around once more to give the customs guy some time to pull someone else over? Or would that look odd?'
Ok, I'm overthinking, just do exactly what I'd do normally.
I got into character, picked the bag up, and was just relieved to have landed so that I could have a cigarette and that's all I'm concerned about.
I set off walking towards the exit and could see that the customs guy was looking towards me.
I was alone and that there was no one else around.

I can picture his face right now as if it was yesterday.
A tall bloke with a big bushy moustache and black curls coming from under a flat policeman-style hat.
He totally reminded me of Edmund Kemper the nutjob serial killer from America.

I was about five metres away from him when he suddenly stepped forward and raised his arm wanting me to stop.

Oh shit... I'm fu...

Suddenly, there was this huge thunderous clatter and some bloke who must have been sent from heaven came out of nowhere with a trolley stacked full of suitcases and boxes upon boxes, and he went barging past me in a hurry.
The good, observant, and might I say excellent customs officer rightly went straight for the noisy dodgy git with the trolley.

And...phew.

Return to Oz

I'd recently broken up with Wanna.
We'd been together for a couple of years, but we were always on and off. Back in the bar, the Thais would call us 'fire and ice' which summed up our relationship perfectly.

Being single in Pattaya is fun but bloody expensive.
I always had girls coming and going, so when I discovered that I had a grand missing from my hidden stash, I wasn't at all surprised.
I was so pissed off with myself.
I had a slight recollection of going to the bank to get it exchanged but the rate was so bad that I just didn't bother.
No way I was gonna lose money with a bad exchange rate, eh reader?
The thing is, I can't remember putting the money back into my secret stash.
So, did I go on the piss and lose it?
Well, there's a good chance of that.
There was only one girl that would stay overnight, Nadia.
She was a real wild one and absolutely loved sex.
Prostitution was totally the right job for her. Getting paid was just a perk, I think.
All said and done though, I just couldn't see her robbing me.
Now I know that will sound quite naïve, but sometimes your gut is right.

So, what now?
Another little run?

My shoulder and arm were a lot better and I had a mate called Bomber, a brickie from Wigan working in Brisbane Australia who said there was always a job for me there so, Brisvegas it was.

Dove art in Brisvegas

Another one of the lads was Jarvis, a young 25-year-old lad from back home who had been on holiday to Pattaya a few times and of course had got the bug.

When I told him where I was going, he asked if he could be my hod carrier.

"Yeah, no probs, I'll check with Bomber, but you should be reyt."

This wasn't my first time working in Australia.
I'd spent a total of six months in Sydney and three months in Perth, so when I got to immigration, they pulled me over thinking, and quite rightly so that I was working.
I'd seen plenty of the TV shows to know that I was in trouble, but I was armed with a lie.
I'd 'borrowed' the persona of a mate from back home in England and used his real life story as my own.

"Mr. Beattie, you've come here to Australia quite a few times, are you working here, sir?"

"Naa mate, I retired a couple of years ago, but I have a few properties that I rent out and I have to check them over."

"Oh? What is your company?"

"No company. I had a small family business with my brother and we had a few properties left to us from our parents and well, that was enough. I sold up and went to live in Thailand. I've loads of mates here so when I have to do all that visa hassle, I stay here for a few months and then back home. It's a nice little break from the missus too."

"Ok mate, sorry to bother you. We just have to check, aye?"

Because my story seemed legit and didn't set off any alarm bells, I didn't get the full-on check that some people get whereby they go into your phone history and bank details etc. Well, thank fuck he didn't check my bank balance because I had just about enough money to stay in a youth hostel and go out on the piss for a couple of weeks.

Soon after my arrival I started playing poker and was smashing it.
The money was rolling in and I was well up, but like I said previously, I still didn't have the money to back up a down period because believe me, they do come, so this wasn't a sustainable option.

I did get a job, but the agent said that he didn't need a labourer, they just wanted brickies, so that left Jarvis hung out to dry. I couldn't do that, so I said,

"OK, no worries, I'll look elsewhere."

I was paying for me and Jarvis with my winnings from poker and was Billy big-timing it.
Eventually, the agent called back and said that they'd take Jarvis on too.

They must have been desperate for brickies, but I was a bit pissed off because I was doing so well at poker.
I just wanted to keep on with this lifestyle but I knew my winning streak wouldn't last, so I bit the bullet.
Every now and then you know ,I get my sensible head on.

We got lucky renting a cool bungalow in Kingston.
It was owned by a nutty English woman who was really nice but a few years earlier, she'd lost her son.
He was murdered after winning $150,000 on the slots.
When he got the first payment of $25K, he bought a new 4x4 and took a few mates out to celebrate.
One of them slit his throat, nicked the car, and was off.

On my first night there It was actually cold in the bedroom and I thought,

aha, nice one, I almost left this bloody cheap sleeping bag at the hostel.

The only reason I'd bought it in India was to give the illusion of a full suitcase when inspected; it's very light but takes up a lot of room.
I had to save as much weight as possible to allow for the chocolate, but I'd never actually used it to sleep in.

I unravelled the bag by flicking it open as you do and heard a small thud on the floor.
Something had dropped out.
I instantly knew what it was and just stood there in utter disbelief.

I was staring at a bundle of wonga.

It was the grand that I'd lost in Pattaya.

I must have stashed it when pissed up in a super-secret hiding place that was so super-secret even I didn't know where it was.

Oh, what a joy.

I wish I hadn't twatted Nadia now...**Joke**...I'm joking.

What I did next would quite unexpectedly come up in the investigation room in Japan.

Ye see, the night before, I won a grand at the casino and had it in $100 black chips, and as I sat outside on the porch smoking a ciggy, still buzzing from finding my missing money and the big win I saw a dead dove with a broken neck on the path.

I'd just bought my first digital camera, only a crappy cheap second-hand one, but I'd started to have myself on as a bit of a David Bailey (who's he?).

I spread out the money in £20 notes above the dead bird and artistically placed the poker chips on and all around this fallen ambassador for peace.

I thought it looked really cool.

So, fast forward into the future and imagine me trying to explain it to a Japanese interrogator when he pulls out a blown-up picture of it.

The Delhi of the Beast

After a couple of months of working our bollocks off and relentlessly being attacked by bastard flies in the crazy heat of Queensland and my back throwing its hand in, we'd had enough.
Just as we had put our hands up and said fair enough, we surrender, bad luck thought,

oh, I'll have a piece of this and kicked us right in the twins.

The bad run at poker eventually came, and on two consecutive nights I hit a full house on the flop only to get 'death by Quads' (sorry to bore the non-poker player). Basically, I lost two grand.

Our three-month visas were up and it was time to move on and I knew exactly what **I** was going to do. But what about Jarvis?
I'd never mentioned about what we were up to back in Thailand. I presumed that he might know because there's always someone who is gonna flap their yap about it when pissed up or whatever, so when I put it to him, I was surprised to hear him say that he didn't know anything about it.

"Haha, you fuckers, me and my mates always wondered how you lot got to stay there for so long, ye dodgy cunts."

I really didn't like getting anyone else involved, especially a young lad.
Imagine him getting caught and the guilt I'd carry with me.

I explained the setup, and he was on board, but only on one condition; that he went with me.
I was completely fine with that as I knew he wouldn't bottle it and fuck it up and I did feel a responsibility for him.

So it was back to Thailand to make some plans.
Nepal first to sort the Visa for India, then on to Copenhagen.

"It's a cockin' doddle," Pete said.

It was great to be back in Kathmandu with no dodgy suitcases to be collected, and this time it was all above board.
Abbie was there too with his wife. He had a Nepalese wife.
I could have sworn he was a poofter.
He took us out to the local casino giving it the big 'I am'.
We got hammered and inevitably couldn't find our hotel.
It took us all frigging night.
We were only there for two days in order to sort out Jarvis's visa.

The plan this time was simple and effective.
We were on our way to Copenhagen to start a new job after our visa for Australia had expired and were taking a quick break visiting the mountains and the Taj Mahal.
A quick look at our passports would confirm all this, so there should be very little explaining to do.

Now previously, I had a little trouble with the hotel staff in India just sticking their nose in and asking really annoying questions such as

'why we got new cases' and 'where from?'
Innocuous enough, I know, but when you've got cases with drugs in them, you don't want pointless questions that could lead to you giving something away.
They almost caught me wanking once because I forgot to lock my hotel room door. They did the old knock and walk in

rather than knocking and waiting.
I mean, what is the point of knocking if you're just going to walk straight in?
This is what they're like.
They only ask the questions about the luggage because they always have an uncle that can get it cheaper.
They really can get on your tits.

So, this time I arranged for the drop-off guy to pick us up at the airport so that we can go straight to the hotel and not give them a reason to start asking questions.

'Can-do' came to pick us up as planned, I was getting to know this guy oh too well.

"Can-do, meet Jarvis, Jarvis... Can-do..."

and then the Can-do show would start.

"Oh yes, Indian ladies... can do, Russian ladies... can do, you want to meet Bollywood superstar?"

We looked at each other. "Er..."

"Old ladies? (He looked at Jarvis) young boys? Can do."

"Reyt, steady on pal."

"I can do that, anything you want, I can do. Hello, I'm Can-do."

The fat fucker couldn't tie his own shoelaces.
I'll tell what he could do, eat like a pig and talk utter shite.

We got dropped off just outside the centre of Delhi in a nice quiet area that I'd checked out the last time I was here. The hotel was fairly small; it only had three floors and as we checked in the receptionist said:

"Oh, it's very quiet today, only you two and one more guest stopping."

Doing that stereotypical bobblehead thing they do.

"The best room is just below and around the corner, sir."

He gave us the key and we went to our room.
It was a decent gaff with plenty of space.

As soon as the door had closed, me and Jarvis looked at each other and sniffed in tandem... sniff, sniff.

"What the fuck?"

I went over to the cases.
It stunk of bush, I mean, the room absolutely reeked of it.

"Fuck this, I'm off," said Jarvis. "We'll never get away with that in an airport."

I wasn't so sure.

"Wait up, wait up. This is bush we're smelling and we're smuggling resin. They don't smell the same; some fucker has had a joint in here or is having one round the back because... "

I sniffed each bag.

"It's not coming from here, have a good whiff yourself. it's just a coincidence."

Oh shit, here I go again,

I went for a little walk around the back of the hotel, hoping to see someone having a crafty smoke.
I played with some street dogs while I thought things through.

I went back to the room with a plan.
A good plan.
A plan that involved drinking and waiting.

"OK, let's put the cases in the bathroom because it was all clear in there. We'll shut the door, have a beer, give it ten, then see."

We sat there for the longest ten minutes. Constantly watching the clock and downing bottles of beer like they were going out of fashion.
We crept up to the door in case the smell could hear us coming.

I don't know, we were under pressure.

We opened it and thankfully, got the all clear.

"See? I told ye, some dodgy Elephant washer is on the wacky baccy!"

The White Mariah

We took just enough money with us for a good meal and a few beers, but as we went zooming down the road in a rickshaw, I said,

"whoa, we've forgotten the bloody hotel card again, it's got the address on it. Go back, go back."

I didn't fancy another night wandering around Delhi like we did the previous night in Kathmandu.

So, it was back around the one-way system and as we were pulling up to the hotel, I told Jarvis,

"leg it in, pal and get two cards just to be safe."
Jarvis was off like a shot to get the cards.
He was eager to get back on track and experience his first big night out in Delhi.

The next 30 seconds were like The Matrix slow motion style shit.
All this happened due to us not paying attention to our surroundings and from information overload.
As I casually turned to watch Jarvis going through the hotel doors it suddenly became blindingly,
shouting in my face,
kick me up the arse obvious,
that the foyer was full of police, and right outside was a big white van with big, huge, block letters…

DELHI POLICE.
Straight away on instinct, I grabbed the side of the door ready to jump out and run to God knows where but I stopped myself when I realised they were ignoring Jarvis.
He briskly, but not in a manner that would suggest;

'OH MY GOD THERE'S COPPERS EVERYWHERE',
picked up the cards and headed back to the rickshaw.

Jumping back in, he said,
"What the fuuuuckkk?"

"Shhh,"

I pointed to the always nosey driver just in front of us.

As soon as we got out and into a bar, we both went into 'oh shit, we're fucked' mode.
My mind was racing,

"Jeez, mate, I thought you hadn't seen em."

"What? Course I saw them. I couldn't fucking miss em. By the time I'd realised, I'd walked through about eight coppers but I was already there, so I just grabbed the cards and played it cool. It didn't help seeing the big van outside.

I mean, I don't know how we both missed it as we pulled up. They must have been able to smell the bags and called the cops."

"Why else would they be there?" I queried. "There's only us and one other guest."
My gut instinct to not leg it was right.
Nothing made sense.
If they were after us, they would have arrested us on the spot. They didn't bat an eyelid when Jarvis just walked through them, in and out of the hotel. Maybe they were all being shit and the police asked the bloke on the desk,

'what do they look like?'
and the guy replied,

'Oh, that's one of them that just walked out'.

Over and over, beer after beer, we went through all the scenarios.
I'll tell you what, it's hard to get pissed in these situations.
I don't know, is it the adrenaline dump?
We didn't have much money on us and NO PASSPORTS.
We could just call Can-do, Abbie, or Pete to get money and fake passports sent to us and get the hell out of Dodge.

Or... just go back and hope for the best.

Or... just one of us go back.

I mean, if it's going tits up, at least one of us has a chance to get out.
I wasn't trying to be the hero and it wasn't that I didn't trust him to do it, because up till now, Jarvis had played it all cool, but I did feel responsible for getting him into this shit show. It could also be just a coincidence.
I had kinda been here before with CID Jim thinking that he was a copper.

Maybe they were there to find the pot smoker?
It absolutely stunk of bush when we got to our room and if we could smell it, then anyone could.
It wasn't from our cases, they were fine.

SO WHY SO MANY COPPERS FOR FUCKS SAKE?

I really hope that you can feel the turmoil that I go through in all these situations that I get myself in to.
Poor me.

"Reyt, Jarvis. I'm going to stake out the hotel and if it looks dodgy, I'll be back and off we go. If all looks good, I'll go in and check out the room rapido. I'll get the money and passports then come back here by... (looking at the time) one o'clock. If I'm not back by then, get the fuck out of here. Get on to Can-do, he'll pay off the police."

Abbie told us that if we ever got into trouble, we had to call Can-do and he would slip some coppers he knew 15K and they would help us, but this had to be done quickly and before the press got wind of it otherwise it would become too big to hush up.

"If that doesn't work, I swear on my kid's life, I won't say fuck all to the police. At a guess, you'll have to go by land over the border back to Nepal, but don't worry, I'll be back before one o'clock pal."

We called each other 'soft cunts' and off I went, back to the hotel.
I was absolutely crapping it as I pulled up around the corner from the hotel.
The streets were dead, there wasn't a soul about.

I was in full Ninja mode.

I was the night.

I saw a pack of dogs that I'd befriended earlier.
Most of them had gone into night mode with that pack mentality going on, but one came bounding over jumping up at me like a long-lost relative.
It was a right scruffy bugger, full of mange and all sorts, but it helped calm me down and I used it to blend in just in case anyone was watching me.

The next thing, the other dogs saw me petting it and thought,

'oh yeah, he's alright let's all go over and say hello.'
So here I am,
'The Shadow',
and the next thing I've got all these bloody dogs jumping up at me trying to lick my face and barking all over the show.
I finally got them to lose interest and continued on in stealth mode.

The police van had gone and I checked all the parked cars in view of the hotel to be sure that no one was staking it out.

I strolled past, kind of like I was lost and wasn't sure if it was my hotel or not, when really, I was just looking for any abnormalities.

I must have walked around the block three times and knew that If anyone was watching me - nosey neighbours are everywhere - I would start to look suspicious.
All looked good.
I had one more smoke while I surveyed the situation and then...

'Bollocks. I'm going for it'.

The hotel receptionist was fast asleep with his head down on the counter which had to be a good sign.

"Excuse me... cough, cough... excuse me."

He woke up in a daze.

"Hello, you alright mate?"

He looked at me like, eh? what do you want?

I thought, *'this fucker is stoned, hmmm, I wonder if...'*

"Keys, mate? There," I said, pointing to our key just behind him.

He shook his head which meant many things.
Yes, no, maybe.
Basically, in India, it fits every scenario, but in this case it meant,

'OK dickhead, let me do my job. I've just been rudely woken up.'

I asked him, just out of interest, why there were a lot of police earlier. Had there been some trouble of sorts?
He had no idea what I was papping on about or... he was the best actor.
When I got into the room, I did a quick memory check, and everything looked just as we'd left it.
I grabbed all the money we had and the passports.
I had a last look inside the cases to see if they had been tampered with in any way, then it was out and back to Jarvis.

It was ten past one after all the messing about, so I was glad to see he'd given me another 15 minutes.
He thought it had all gone south and was basically clinging on to the hope that I had been delayed.
My God, the look on his face when he saw me. He threw his head back giving it,

"Thank God."

When I got closer, I could see he had tears in his eyes, we gave each other a big, manly, cuddle.

The British Passport.

At check in we were in separate queues and as Jarvis was checking in, the woman dealing with him was being way too inquisitive and it looked like she didn't believe him.
It's got fuck all to do with her, these are questions Immigration should be asking.

"Why only go to Nepal for three days?"

"Well, mainly for my visa. Nepal was the only place I could get a visa for India in such a short time, so I thought great, while I'm here, I'll go and see Mount Everest."

"But why come to India for only five days?"

I could see and hear everything and was starting to get a little worried.

"What? I've just been to Agra, the Taj Mahal. For two days." With a slight chuckle in his voice, he continued:
"So I'm going to Nepal to see the most famous mountain on Earth and came to India to see one of the wonders of the world, and you wonder why?"
She still didn't look happy but Jarvis played it well, got his ticket, and was off.
Now, I had a little dilemma because I basically had the same story and answers, so if I was to be questioned in the same way, then should I just change my story now?
Like right now in my head?
There's no way I could come up with anything convincing in such a short time so I just stuck to the plan.

Thankfully, it was a different lady checking me in and no silly questions about where I'd been, but then...

"Sir, why do you have two passports?"

"Pardon?"

I had no idea what she was on about. She showed me the front cover of my passport and pointed to Britain and

Northern Ireland.
She asked again.

"Sir, why are there two countries?"

I was a bit gobsmacked.

"Erm… no… it's just one."

To be honest, I'd never realised it said that on the cover, I thought it just said, 'Great Britain'.

"OK, wait here, sir."
Like I had any choice.

She went over to the main guy and I could see her explaining the **glaring irregularity** and could also see him looking at her like the silly twat that she had just made of herself.
He came over waving my passport in the air.

"I'm so sorry my good sir, this is the number one passport in the world and **this?**… this is a bloody fool," pointing to the now very timid checkout girl.
I looked over at her and gave the Stan Laurel nod.
'Hmm, mm'.

Wonderful, Wonderful Copenhagen

Straight out through customs and not a uniform in sight. Oh, such joy to have a simple life.

Jarvis was a computer-savvy young un. When we were in India, he googled hotels in Copenhagen and looked for somewhere for us to stay in the city, and because we were still playing the part of travelling solo, we arranged to meet at a designated hotel; he'd even shown me a photo of the hotel. I was pretty impressed with this electrickery.

I was even more impressed when we were in Australia and Jarvis took me to a kind of cybercafé in the shopping mall. This was back in 2007 and it was the first time I'd seen social media. Jarvis got onto a computer and was showing me round this new Facebook thing, and he was telling me how it was really good for getting birds and that lot.
Kinda like Friends Reunited.
Looking around me, I could see that this was very popular.

"I think this might catch on."

The place was packed. He said,

"Look, Cyrus has sent me a message."
and he clicked on it.
 The next thing, (it must have been the first ever porn bomb) all these screams of ecstasy came blaring out.
Everyone was looking at us and Jarvis was freaking out giving it,

"I can't turn it off, I can't turn it off... He's fucking done me!"
It just seemed to be getting louder and louder.
I was laughing my arse off and just said,

"I'll leave you to it." as I walked off.

Cyrus the virus

This man is the technological mastermind behind the whole thing. Without this computer colossus, there would be no story.
He was sharp, had a keen mind, and was always one step ahead.
There was no code he couldn't crack.

He was called Nigel, was from Wolverhampton, and I wouldn't trust him to sit the right way round on a toilet.

Nigel was a bit like the 'Rain Man'.
Remember the film with Dustin Hoffman?
Yeah... kinda like that.
He was shit hot on the computer though, and must have been one of the earliest pioneers of computer hacking.
He would hack into big American corporate companies, who at the end of the month would suss that they had been hacked, so claimed the money back off the insurance companies.
So really, it was the insurance companies that were getting screwed and I won't lose any sleep over that.

We would fly all over the world in business class and the likes of us mixing with the hoity-toity was a scene to behold.

I remember on one trip, one of Abbie's henchmen, Azar, wanted to come with us just for a holiday.
He was a big seven-foot Middle Eastern bloke who ticked all the boxes for being a James Bond bad guy.
He was a big dopey fucker in actuality, but a really nice guy and we had many a good laugh with him.

Well, on this particular trip, we were coming back from the Philippines from a long weekend break and Azar fell asleep pissed up. So, me being the opportunist that I am, got hold of a black marker pen and wrote 'TERRORIST' on his forehead.
He didn't realise until we got to the hotel.
He had walked all the way through customs with it.
He was not happy.

So, here I am, assessing the situation in Copenhagen.
Taxi to hotel… no problem.
Check to see if he had got there first… nope… no problem.
Chill in the fresh air, enjoy the sunlight, and pollute lungs with cigarettes… no problem.
40 minutes later… Where the bloody hell is he?
Problem.
I got a new Danish SIM card and called Pete.

"All went well except Jarvis hasn't arrived at the hotel… which he picked, and it's definitely the right hotel."
Pete told me,

"Reyt, just get out of there and find a new hotel and hopefully Jarvis will ring me."

Thankfully, he did and had just got lost in the airport and ended up catching the train, which ended up taking a lot longer than just jumping in a cab.
Just when ye think it's simple, eh.

Stealing the bag/Burning bridges

The last two times I did a run, the little voice inside that everyone has when you're doing something wrong, was telling me that I need to stop doing this.
I was stuck in a loop, and I knew that the only way out was by getting caught or making a run no longer an option.

'Why not just stop?' I hear you say.

Well, that's OK when you have money, but the money will soon run out and then the reality of having to go back to the UK to work until I could afford to come back compared to just doing a quick run would become a no-brainer.
I mean, that's how I ended up doing this in the first place.

The only way to put a stop to this before it was too late, was to take away the option of a quick fix and the way to do that was to screw Abbie over and sell the bag to some dodgy git that I'd most likely meet in whichever city I'd end up in.

I remember back in Pattaya, there was an old hippy guy that used to play chess with Pete.
I can't remember his name, but he was quiet and kept himself to his self but we all knew he was in on the game.

One day, Pete told me that he reckoned he had done one. He landed at the airport with a bag and that was it, no one ever saw him again.
He hadn't been caught, he just dropped completely off the radar.

Looking back, one of my few regrets was not doing exactly that.

Pattaya Bar Girls P.I.

I had this idea floating around my head for a while after seeing and hearing many a tale of 'The Sick Buffalo', which incidentally was another nickname of mine that the Thais had given me.
Farang Kwai' - foreign buffalo after a few brief, but painful, attempts at riding them.

I digress, I had this idea to expose the girls that were fleecing the customers… sorry… boyfriends.

So, let me set the scene.
It's your standard Thai love story of foreigner meets Thai bar girl. They fall in love, he goes back home, promises to take care of her so she doesn't have to work the bar anymore, she goes back home, saving herself for his return, and they all live happily ever after. Awwwww.

I had one of those lightbulb moments when I was having an intimate moment, doggy style with Nadia.
Nadia was the complete professional.
She had three or four phones, and they all had a little flag on them which was the nationality of the boyfriend.
That way, if the boyfriend looked through the phone, it all seemed legit and obviously, she would never say the wrong name when she answered.

The phone rang and she turned around putting her finger up to her lips and said to me,

"Shh , slowly, slowly, it's boyfriend number two....Hello baby, I miss you too much!"
Can you believe this girl?
She doesn't even tell me to stop while she's talking to her 'boyfriend'.
That's when I thought this place needs a....
        (cue Magnum P.I. music) ...

PRIVATE INVESTIGATOR.

I had to find a way of legally being able to make a living in Thailand, and I really didn't fancy buying a bar or teaching English which seemed to be the main options at the time and smuggling wasn't a long-term plan.
I mean, the bubble had to burst.
So, I set up...

Pattaya Bar Girls P.I.:
'Check her out before The Damage is Done'.

I got a mate to set up a website and I got a shitload of cards and stickers done.

Believe it or not, but only two days ago as of writing this, I saw one of my flyers on a beachfront lamppost.

So, I went to town, got a cool hat and some shades and I was back with my sidekick. The Silverback.
I got a new phone and number and sat waiting for the first call.
I'd set the Magnum theme tune as my ringtone of course.

There were a few of us drinking beers at Smix's shop cum bar in Coronation Street.
It wasn't really called this but, because there where so many northerners there, it just seemed to be the obvious name for it.

If there were ever any domestics on the street, then everyone would start singing the Coronation Street theme tune.

We were all having a good crack when suddenly, the Magnum theme tune started playing. It was my phone. We all stopped and looked at each other.

"Right... fuck off. Who's taking the piss?"

We all cracked up.
I knew there was a good chance this was a windup, but I legged it across the road, took a breath, and composed myself while trying not to laugh.

"Hello, Pattaya P.I. speaking, how may I help?"

A well-spoken English chap answered; this accent was too good to be a wind up, none of my mates were that good.

"Hi, could I possibly meet you somewhere? It's quite personal and..."

"Ok, stop right there. The less said, the better. Time and place?"

"Em, later today. 4pm at em... The Tahitian Queen?"

"Ok, go to the right-hand side of the bar and buy a Pina colada. I'll find you."

I know, I know, Pina Colada? I don't know where that came from. It's all I could think of on the spot.

I felt as though I was in my own version of the classic series, Magnum P.I.

Episode 1.
THE PRICE OF LOVE.

Bob was an older guy in his early 70s from London town. He still worked at some company as a managing director both here in Thailand and in the Philippines, and that's where he met his stunning, and I mean stunning, 27-year-old wife.

They had been married for a year and he brought her over to live in Pattaya. She was a smart cookie in one way or another and within a year, she was fluent in Thai, had her own floral business, and everyone loved her, especially the local police captain who Bob was absolutely convinced was knobbing her.

"I want you to bug my house and find out for sure what's going on."

"Ok Bob, I need to clarify a bit more." I was straight with him from the off.

"Here's the deal. All I do is I catch the bar girls out when they say they're going home but really they're staying in the bar and most importantly, I don't go up against the police here."

"No, I get it, I really do, but I need help, and I know the chief of police personally through my business connections here in Pattaya."

"Sorry Bob, I really don't want to get involved with the police here, they are extremely corrupt and very dangerous. I advise you to tread very carefully my friend."

"I'll pay you whatever you want."

"I'll bug the house tomorrow."

I went to Tukcom, the well-known electric gadget complex in south Pattaya. Its mental the stuff you can buy there.

I bought a tiny, hidden camera for five thousand baht (£100). Bob was fine with paying for any special equipment that I may need and didn't bat an eyelid when he got the receipt for 10,000 baht... nice.

I met him the day after I got my first recording, but you couldn't see anything.
You could just hear them chatting for about an hour.

The reason why Bob got suspicious in the first place was because he'd been paying the security guard to keep an eye on her. He wasn't that stupid.
A gorgeous young woman with a fat old rich bloke?
He was suspicious as fuck.

So, when the security guard told him that the captain had been coming round pretty much every day and she never so much as mentioned it. Well... That's when he smelt a rat.

Me and Wanna, yes, I call her Wanna when I need her help, listened to the whole thing and translated word for word what was said.
It all seemed like fairly normal chitchat, but what we did get out of it was that she was 100% Thai and from Buriram.
The same place as Wanna.

Buriram has a local dialect which is a mix of Khmer and Thai with it being so close to the border of Cambodia, and If she had learned Thai with a Khmer accent in a year, then... yeah... right. Well, there was just no way... end of.

Bob would have none of it. He was insistent.

"I met her in the Philippines and I also met her family. So, she might have somehow..."

"No way, Bob."

I asked a few of the local women to listen to her accent and everyone said the same thing. She was either from Buriram or somewhere in Esaan, but definitely Northeast Thailand.

At a guess, I would say she was well clued-up and was on some kind of blag in the Philippines.
She had dug herself into a hole with all her lies to Mr. Money Bags and maybe had to pay off a poor fake family to catch a big fish?
It all sounds a bit extreme but whaddya reckon? ....No?
Well, you have a go.

After three days of doing nothing but filling my pockets, Bob rang me and said:

"No need to translate this one, Mr. D (as I'd named myself). They were at it like rabbits. It was loud and clear."

"Bob, don't overreact and do what I told you. Go straight to your friend the chief of police. Please Bob, let them sort it out and don't, I repeat don't, say you hired a private investigator."

Part of me felt sorry for the old fool but I was angrier with myself.

WHY DIDN'T I ASK HIM TO GIVE ME THE VIDEO TAPE AS EVIDENCE?
She really was hot.

I checked in on him a couple of weeks later just to see how he was doing, and he had forgiven her of course and she promised to never do it again...Of course.

Episode 2.
THE BLIND ALASKAN TWINS.

Texas Mike's best buddy Shaun had just been scammed by his wife, so he called in the big guns.

Erm?   Me.

He'd heard about my new enterprise in the Jack o' Tar where we'd all hang out and he told me all about her shenanigans.

Shaun and Scott were a pair of virtually blind, tobacco chewing, identical twins from Alaska that lived in Pattaya. They both had some hereditary illness that would eventually blind them. Scott had already retired due to his loss of sight, but Shaun could still work from a computer and was working for some big oil company.
He was a bargirl's crock of gold.

Texas Mike gave me the rundown.

The wife said that she got mugged for 20,000 baht (£300 back then) and the thief took all her gold rings, necklaces, and most importantly, their grandmother's ring.

"Scott and I ain't buying it and we ain't got a goddamn clue what we can do about it."
He continued,

"Shaun is back next week and he don't know shit as yet. Whaddya think, Dam'arge?"

I would change my nickname when introduced as Damage to Dam'arge, saying it was from the French side of the family. I figured that it sounded softer on the ears to the ladies... more romantic, No?
Anyway, for many, it just stuck.

"OK, Mike, I'm on it, get me her phone number, full name and any nicknames. I need her address here and out in the sticks or wherever she's from. I want the addresses of all the places that she's worked since living here in Pattaya. Oh, and all the info about as many of her friends as you can get. You got it?"

I think Mike was quite impressed, and so was I if I do say so myself. Mike told me,
"OK, just get the ring back buddy. We know the rest has most likely gone. Scott will replace the money and the jewellery; he just doesn't want his brother to know what's happened and get hurt."

I had a good talk with Wanna about what she thought had gone on and she came to the same conclusion as me.

We reckoned that her Thai husband most likely wanted more money than what she was giving him.
He more than likely got pissed on the Lao Khoa (local brew), gave her a kicking, and just took it all off her.
She was on a really good earner with Shaun, so doing a fake robbery was her only chance to explain away everything.

I drove to her and Shaun's swanky condo with my other little side kick, Daadam (black eyes), a street dog that had befriended me.
I was quickly turning into a 1980s American detective show with my two sidekicks, the Gorilla and the Soi dog.

We sort of adopted Daadam and brought her into our little

apartment and she loved it and us.

She'd follow me everywhere, and when I got on my bike, she would jump on the back and lean on me with her paws on my shoulder.

So here I was, about ten floors up and just about to knock, when suddenly the door opened, and this foreign guy came out followed by Shaun's wife.

She had absolutely no idea who I was, but I had seen photos of her and had the advantage.

"Mrs Morrison? I'm Mr. D, a private investigator sent from America by your husband's family. We need to talk."

Her companion spoke up.

"Who the fuck's this cunt?"

Using my detective skills, I quickly established he was Scottish.

She was gobsmacked and, as I spoke to the Jock, she turned white.

"Oreyt pal, sorry about this, it looks like she's had you off as well. She's married to an American guy who's working offshore but her 'real' Thai husband has taken all her money and jewellery, so she has said that she was mugged in order to keep her American husband none the wiser.

The family want the police involved and want to press charges, but I've asked them to give me two days to sort it. If the police get involved, she could be looking at a long prison sentence".

He was just as surprised as her and was quite visibly upset. He wouldn't have it at first and said that there must be some mistake and said the classic:

"She's not a bar girl."

You could see the turmoil and realisation going on in his head.

This was a classic case of,

'You'll never get me falling for those bar girl scams, I've been here too long, I know the game. This girl is different; she loves me'.

He was a mix of rage, heartbreak, and embarrassment.
I really did feel sorry for him but didn't say anything.
He didn't need to hear it. He'd seen this happen to other guys before and now he was in the sucker club.
He looked at her, but she couldn't look back at him.
She knew she was busted, and he knew he'd been shafted.
He slowly walked off just shaking his head in disbelief.
The bluff totally worked.
She didn't even attempt to get out of it. She did try the fake cryng, but I just said,

"Look, you still have a chance, yeah?"
She stopped crying and looked at me.

"Give me your husband's number and my Thai operative will call to arrange a pickup of the grandmother's ring. That's all the family want. OK? Shaun will know nothing of this, get rid of the boyfriend and tell the husband to keep a low profile or he will go to jail next time. And you? You're being watched."

The Silverback was well on it, she spoke to the husband, and not only did she come back with the ring, but all the jewellery too.

The dog did fuck all.

I later saw the Scottish guy in a bar, and he bought me a drink and apologised for 'bein' a cunt.'
I told him he had nothing to apologise for.
He wasn't the first and he won't be the last.
I just gave him my card and said,

"Next time, just call me before the damage is done."

Cue the Magnum music.

Episode 3.
THE SOLDIER

I got a call from a guy called Simon (Smudge), another English guy that once again needed to meet face-to-face as it was all too complicated.

This time I asked what he would be wearing, none of that Pina Colada bollocks.
We met at Jameson's, an Irish pub just five minutes from where I lived.
I spotted his West Ham top straightaway, and we both acknowledged each other.
I got a pint of Guinness and heard his story.

He was in some special forces outfit or something (he never said, and I never asked which) on an operation in Afghanistan that went horribly wrong.

Twelve men were on their way to some secret mission and Smudge being in the back, asked his friend if they could swap seats while he spoke to his mate, the driver.

BOOM.

They were hit with an RPG and all ten in the back were killed. Only Smudge and the driver survived, barely.

He showed me his head, and a quarter of his skull was missing.
As I looked at the huge dent in his head, I caught myself thinking,

'If he stands in the rain with no hat on, he'll end up with a puddle in his head.'

I know, it's mental to think something like this, but these thoughts just come to me, and I really can't help it.
At least I don't say them out loud... anymore.

Smudge was in a coma for many months and four years later, he was still suffering and very confused.

He told me how his brother took complete control of everything while he was under.
Cutting all ties with Thailand and just focusing everything on helping him with his recovery. It was a miracle he survived and as he was telling me his story, tears were in his eyes.

He remembered all his mates that he lost that day and the deepest cut was the fact his mate's wife blamed him for her husband's death because they swapped seats.
Such a cruel twist of fate and even when he finally got to the point of seeing her after years of recovery, she still blamed him.
Ridiculous I know, but I guess the fact that Smudge had no kids and now her kids had no father still burned, and it was just easier to direct that pain at him.

He did remember going to Thailand years before and having a great time, but it was all very vague, and he couldn't remember anything else.

After many years of recovery, he came back to Thailand and was having a great time when one evening he just walked into a random bar and all the girls went crazy.

The Mamasan saw Smudge and shrieked,

"OH MY BUDDHA. SALMON (Thais can't say simon), YOU COME BACK."

He had no idea who she was.

"Hey, we not see you long time, why you go? No come back, Lek she crazy, you cheat her."

Lek?

He was so confused and had absolutely no idea what she was on about. He told me,

"They couldn't understand how I didn't remember any of them and thought I was being weird. I ended up getting really frustrated with them. Since the incident happened, I don't handle things very well at all, to say the least. I kept going over the name in my head and then suddenly, the memories rushed back, it nearly floored me."

He explained how he asked about Lek and then with a quick look and a snap from the Mamasan, everyone fell silent. Everyone was confused and the Mamasan was trying to weigh up the situation and didn't want to drop her into any kind of trouble.

The penny dropped.

"Lek... is my wife... She's my wife."

Once that piece of the puzzle came back to him, everything else fell into place.
He remembered Noi, she was a good pool player and was Lek's best friend.

He continued,

"Of course, this was her bar where we drank almost every night. I don't know why but they all just stopped talking to me. I went back to my room to get my medal to prove my story and pointed out the big fucking dent in my head, but they just didn't understand. I was so frustrated and angry, I just threw my medal at the bar and left."

Before I continue, I will have to confess that I can't remember what medal he had received.
I do remember saying,

"bloody hell that's impressive."
But he just replied,

"for what? Surviving while all my mates died?"
He told me,

"I just wanted to know what had happened to her. I called my brother yesterday and he filled me in with what he knew."

His brother and the rest of the family thought Smudge would most likely not make it and just didn't tell Lek, thinking she was just a holiday girlfriend.
For some reason, he never told them he was married to Lek.

"So, yesterday I saw your poster on a lamp post and well, here I am. Can you help?"

I was quite taken aback by his story and I really wanted to get him his medal back, as well as his wife.

I was telling my mate, Aussie Dave aka 'The flamin' Galah, about the whole thing and he said,

"I know that bladdy baa, you need a partner mate?"
Aussie Dave was a mate from the early days of Soi 4 at 'Arry's bar. Dave took me to the Wonderland which was a bar at the top end of Soi 13 and I started the clock (I was charging one thousand Baht - £15 quid - per hour).

We started playing pool and I asked for the best player they had, which I already knew was Lek's best friend Noi.

I knew the game they played very well but this time I was the one fishing.
Like an angler fish I lured her in with the chance of a quick buck for bait.

I started the ball rolling.

"Hey, I remember you from a few years ago, yeah?"

"Oh yes, wow good to see you... you buy me dink?"

They really don't mess about when they know they can get money out of you.

Me and Ozzy Dave spent the next two hours craftily trying to gain as much info as possible, talking to the Mamasan and even getting lots of 'dinks' in, but to no avail.
I started to think that maybe, because of the brain damage, Smudge had actually got it all wrong.
So, I called him and asked him to come to the bar, just to explain everything to the Mamasan and hopefully, with me translating the best I can, get to the bottom of it.
Aussie Dave thought that was a good idea too.

After 15 minutes, I called him again.

"Hi mate, you ok?"

"Yeah, I'm at the bar now talking to the Mamasan."

I had a good look around, knowing damn well he wasn't in the bar that we were in as there was only a few people in.
I asked Noi the pool player.

"What's the name of this bar?"

"Wonderland."
And then she added,

"Two...Wonderland original round corner."
Oh, shit a brick, we were in the wrong frigging bar.
Dave, ye really are a Flaming Galah.
It was at the end of the next soi along, 13/1. We legged it round to the right Wonderland and Smudge was already falling out with the staff.
After calming things down and explaining the situation to the Mamasan, she told how Lek thought he had just gone off with another woman.
She was absolutely heartbroken but moved on and eventually met and married another Farang. They had a couple of kids and now lived somewhere in Germany.

I did get him his medal back and he finally got closure and it was another case solved.
I didn't charge him for our time in the wrong bloody bar.

A bit of an anti-climax I know, but life isn't all Hollywood endings.

One Last Job

I was really enjoying being a private detective.
It was fun, exciting, and quite promising, but alas, such is life that if you do something you enjoy, it never pays well.
I was running out of money and over the next few weeks, it would be gone faster than a toupee in a hurricane.

I had a few setbacks that really put me on my arse.

I ran into the back of a car with my motorbike when a dog ran out in front of the car ahead of me and he had to slam his brakes on. It was my fault so had to sort it out Thai style which cost me 20,000 Baht.

My neck injury had come back so I was getting treatment in the hospital which involved me getting my neck stretched.
I had to have a special massage.
(not that kind you dirty-minded sod; it was a sports massage).
I also had electro acupuncture which was expensive but seemed to work in releasing trapped nerves.

Also, and I've been dreading writing this bit… there was Wanna.

We were having one of our silly little arguments in the flat when she suddenly grabbed a steak knife.

I was out the door like a shot shouting at her to calm down.
Mad that, isn't it?
When you shout at people telling them to calm down?
Ah… the things you do when you think you're going to get stabbed to death.
We weren't even drunk, for fuck's sake.

I was just leaving and as I was closing the door, I heard a grunting noise.
It was an eerie, guttural sound that sounded out of place from the usual temper tantrums.
It was like a muted kind of violence, and it wasn't directed at me.
Something was wrong… very wrong.

I paused for a few seconds and decided to go back in to see what was going on.
I slowly opened the door, fearful that she was baiting me and was going to make a lunge for me as soon as I stepped inside.
The door was not even halfway opened when I could see the dark red blood on the floor tiles spreading out like a scene from a horror movie with Wanna face down in it.
I could see straight away it was from her wrist.
She'd hacked so hard at her wrist that her hand looked like it was hanging off.

I screamed for help from anyone that might be about as I pulled off a thick rubber band from a thousand-pound bundle, cursing as the money flew about everywhere like a tickertape parade, but I didn't give a shit.
I doubled up on the elastic band to stem the flow of blood and wrapped a towel around it, then carried her down the stairs to my bike.
I somehow managed to drive her to the nearest hospital in soi 5.

They took her in and thankfully stopped the bleeding, but because it was a private hospital, they told me it would cost at least 200,000 baht (Three grand GBP then) for such a major operation.
I just didn't have that kind of money, so they said,

"Take her to Banglamung local Hospital where it is free for Thais."

She was in surgery for nine hours and when she recovered, she was physically OK but mentally was still suffering.
I was becoming increasingly worried about her.
When she wasn't trying to kill me, she really was a wonderfully loving, funny, honest woman, but my God, when she went nuts, she did it in style.

I remember one night we got into a stupid drunken row. It just came out of nowhere and she went absolutely fucking mental. It got to the point that I had to physically hold her down on the bed, and all while the bloody door to the apartment was open and people would just wander past.

Finally, Scotty turned up singing the theme tune to Coronation Street and I saw my out.

"Alright mate?"
I'd put on my best 'everything is just fine' face.
Laughing he said,

"Aye, no worries. Women, eh?"
As he saw me struggling with this spitting lunatic, I said,

"Just take over for a sec, will ya? I'm bursting for a piss."
He gave me a look like 'you want me to deal with that?'

I shouted,
"COME ON, YA CUNT, I'M FUCKING BURSTING."

He reluctantly sprang into action.

"OK, OK, hurry up for fuck's sake."

We had to be careful that she didn't get free and turn into the Tasmanian Devil off the cartoon.
So, with some careful limb restraint deployment, we managed to swap places.
I stood up and exhaled a long thankful 'glad that was over' breath.

"Reyt, cheers pal, I'm off."

"WHAT?"

Laughing, I said,
"I can't hang around here, pal, I've got things to do."

I made my exit singing the theme tune to Coronation Street.
I'd gotten my revenge on him for Mumbai.

"I'll get you some rupees, pal."

I walked away to the shrieks of Scotty calling me every name under the sun and the torrent of abuse from the raging pandemonium that he was sat on.

Just a couple of weeks after 'the wrist incident', shall we call it, and still with the bandage on her wrist that I had to clean twice a day, she got drunk and felt so ashamed about what she did that she tried jumping off the balcony.
Fucking nuts.

Wanna always hated that I had anything to do with smuggling and always said,

"don't think for a minute that if you get caught, I'll wait for you."

Then she went and bought me a little gold Travelling Buddha to guide me on the way.

This was Wanna to a tee.

Such a big-hearted caring woman, and although she didn't want me doing it, she did want me to be safe.

So, I thought I'd do one last job and let's make it a big un and go out with a bang.

Japan was still on the cards, and I'd get a lot more money.

For only two kilos, I'd get $10,000.

Now, that would sort me out fine.

Wanna had stopped drinking, and I had calmed down the party lifestyle a lot.

We had our nice little cosy apartment and a dog.

Me and Jake (One of the lads who convinced me to do the Amsterdam run) got chatting and decided to go together to India and although we would be on the same flight to Japan, we would travel separately.

I had a lot more faith in Jake than Mad Scotty.

My ingenious cover story for the over inquisitive customs officer this time was that I was going to visit my sister who lived and worked for The British Chamber of Commerce in Tokyo.

Together we were going on Holiday to Hokkaido, which is the northmost volcanic island in Japan.

I'd always wanted to go to the hot springs where the monkeys bathe and... erm... ye buying this crap?

Yep?

OK, onward.

From Bombay, to Santa fe, over the hills and far away.

Back to Mumbai, formally known as Bombay.
This was late October 2008, and in the following month there were a series of terrorist attacks on the city killing 175 people.
So, remember all the police in the hotel previously when me and Jarvis thought we'd been rumbled?
Yeah, the police knew something was going to happen and were trying to prevent it, hence all the coppers in the hotel. See?
It all makes sense when you find out these things... five years later.

Again, Goa was the place to chill.
I started to get the feeling that my luck was running out whilst playing poker with Jake down on the beach.
We would play nearly every day and I soon sussed that if I got Jake to sit with his back to the sun, I could see right through the cheap cards we'd bought.
Yes.

Genius, I know.

I couldn't lose, but I bloody well did.

I knew what cards he had and the only unknown was the last card to be turned over from the deck and it would always kick me right in the balls. The only card that he could win with would be turned and I would just stare at it, shaking my head in disbelief whilst Jake would be laughing away, patting himself on the back for a game well played.

It most certainty is a coincidence, but it does affect your mindset.

I've always had the belief that if you think you are lucky you will attract good luck and vice versa, and I really didn't need a seed of doubt growing inside my head.

I got to know and enjoy Goa a lot more this time and I met the famous (in his own head) Goan snake charmer, Avi, who was another one of these can-do fuckers.

He was head of security at Tito's nightclub and was trying to come across as a Mafioso Billy big-time number.

It always strikes me as amazing that I attract and get attracted to these kinds of people. Birds of a feather I guess. I always think,

he / she looks kind of interesting I wonder what their story is.
And I guess they look at me and think,

he looks like he can do a bit, I'll try to impress him with my bullshit.
Especially now, as I was no longer in disguise (I wasn't wearing my glasses).

He told me how he was looking after an English girl who had spent some time in prison after her boyfriend had left her high and dry following a failed drug smuggling caper.
He was giving her food and shelter and trying to get her on her feet until she got a flight back home.

He took me hunting (herping) for cobras, and with him being the cobra king of Goa it should have been quite the adventure, but we seemed to be looking in all the wrong places, poking around trees and bushes.
That's when it twigged (ahem).
He was full of shit.
I thought, *reyt, I'll have him.*

So, when he was poking around in a bush looking for a deadly cobra, I grabbed his ankle and made a hissing sound like a snake and he went from head of security Mr. Mafia to screaming like a girl.
A good boo always uncovers the truth.

A little tip for you here; if you ever want to check if someone is a ladyboy, forget all that looking for the Adams apple etc., just boo 'em.
The natural, deep, 'OH…YA FUCKING DICKHEAD' retort will give them away.
When you boo a bloke, it brings the girl out and when you boo a ladyboy, it brings the bloke out.
Funny that, int it?
Holiday over, it was time to get to work.

Rather than do the easy flight back to Mumbai, we went via a 13-hour train ride to see and embrace more of the country. Once again, I was of the thinking that this could be my last experience of freedom. It didn't disappoint.

We got a second-class sleeper which was more than fine, sharing a compartment with a lovely Indian couple and their two kids that thankfully, although they were giddy at first, just slept for most of the trip.
Ye know that feeling of,
'Oh no, not squawking brats for the whole journey'.

The views were spectacular and I was in awe as we wound our way through the mountains with the countless waterfalls and tunnels. I could sit in-between the carriages cowboy style, drinking cold beer and smoking Marlboro cigarettes while soaking it all up. Taking deep breaths and inhaling the contradiction of fresh mountain air and Marlboro red… aaahhhhh, freedom.

The sunset was a magnificent red glow in the sky but if there's one thing better than a sunset, it's a sunrise.
They're both the perfect times to reflect on life's many ups and down.
Reflection and realisation swamped me whilst in my splendid isolation.
This little run to Japan was no walk in the park and the consequences could be severe.
I knew I had to get my shit together and go home… to see my kids. Watching a normal family really made me realise how much I missed them.
It was eating me up inside, but I'd never let it show.
Eee… I wish I could go back and give myself a good shake.

Slumdogs

It was late at night when we pulled into the main train station but it was still utter chaos. It felt like everyone was on to you for one thing or another.

"Taxi? Hotel? Food? Cigarettes? Water? Tea? Coffee?" Beggars and blaggers of all kinds.
I now know where the phrase, 'sweating like a Bombay baggage handler' comes from.

We got a taxi to our Hotel in Santa Cruz, which is a market area of the city, but as this knobhead was driving off, me and Jake instantly glared at each other.

"Fuck's sake."

He was all over the place and clearly pissed.

"Whoa, mate, slow down, no rush, eh?"

We were completely ignored by Mr. Schumacher sahb and because the roads were quieter, he would go faster and faster and was swerving around the corners like he was in a Bollywood version of 'Smokey and the Bandit'.
We had both been in many an arse-clenching tuk tuk ride, but this was out of control and as soon as he had to make a stop, Jake jumped out and grabbed his key.
I thought he was going to twat him, so I jumped in and tried to calm things down, but this pissed-up fucker was going mad now and wanting his money.

"My. Fucking. Arse."

We just took our bags and flagged down the next taxi.

Jeez, welcome back to Mumbai, the gateway to India or heaven depending on who you get a taxi with.

We got settled into our hotel and waited to hear from Abbie. When he did call, things just didn't seem right.

'Hey, motherfuckers,'
was his normal greeting; imagine a rather camp fella trying to sound all rough and toughie.

In a very straightforward mannerism he just said,

"New plan, I want you to go on separate days just to make sure."

"Make sure of what?" said Jake.

"Well, it's safer that way."

"Safer? How? Is there something we don't know Abbie?" I asked.

"No, no, no, it's just that… well, two years ago, I did have two guys get caught in Japan and because they went together, one grassed the other up. He was nabbed because he had a shit fake passport. That's why I only use the Chinaman. Perfect passports every time. They got two years for four kilos and another two years for incorrect passports, so best you separate please. That way, if one gets caught, the other can abort the run."

Hmmm, this didn't sound right at all.
Hey, what happened to nobody ever getting caught, eh?
Not once did we ever think that it had anything to do with Big Gary.

Six weeks earlier, another one of the crew, Gaz, AKA Big Gary from Sarf London, came to see me and asked if I wanted to make more money and added,

"It's got sweet FA to do with them Sand Wogs, mate."

I could be wrong but I think that Gary is a bit racist.
He'd been in the game for a couple years now had done many a little run, but he'd had enough of being the mule and wanted to be the muleteer.
I could see where he was coming from.

It's just natural to want to move up the ladder, but this isn't the kind of game where you get employee of the month awards. When you want to move up in this game, it inevitably means that someone has to give way.

Big Gary had got pally with the Johannesburg lot and was drawing up plans to screw over the sand wo... erm, Iranians.

"Mate, this is gonna go tits up," I told him.
He also only wanted to deal in Crystal Meth AKA Diamonds as we all know by now.

Then we'd heard via the Pattaya bongo drums that he'd sent a guy off to do a job in South Africa. It was a fella that we knew called Trevor who was an older bloke and a seasoned veteran of the runs. Me and Pete were not happy with this and arranged to have a meeting with Big Gary at a fishing park we all used to frequent. I got straight to the point.

"Mate, word's soon got around that you've sent Trev to Johannesburg. I've fucking told you this lot will not let you get away with it."

"Fuck em. Why should they get all the cream and we get a pittance while taking all the risk?"

It always seems easy when all the hard work has been done, doesn't it?

Big Gaz couldn't grasp the fact that the Iranians had been doing this for years. They had to go through all the pain of getting it wrong to get it right, setting up the contacts, paying off police and security, and then in comes Big Gaz years later, giving it 'piece o' piss this I want some of it'.

They had set up a network all over the world and now Billy big bollocks here seems to think he can just step all over their toes with no consequence.

Pete's turn, and he went at it with a different approach.

"Get that old cunt back from Africa on the next plane. If you want to set up on your own, no problem, good luck, I wish you all the best and if you get it going, superb, then maybe we can do some business. But I've been involved with the Iranians for six years now and they've been nothing but good, honest, criminals and you doing this is gonna fuck everything up and make it'll look really bad on me."

"yeah but th..."

Pete stopped him right in his tracks.

"Get that cunt back. I want to see his passport as soon as he lands and if I hear **anything,** about fucking over Abbie, **you**, ye fat twat, will be going one way fishing next time. Do you understand?"

Pete had ginger power and could be quite persuasive.

The coin flip of density

Both me and Jake had got very used to how things worked. We'd both done many a run and had over time perfected our technique, so we really didn't like the change.

We spoke to Pete and asked if it was anything to do with Big Gary sticking his oar in, but he'd heard nowt, so we felt a lot better. I mean, it does make sense to go on our own;

Just imagine if either me or Curtis had got caught on our run to Japan. They would obviously search whoever they would be travelling with and that's it, both busted.

We got the suitcases, and they were bang on as per. Two, identical, pristine, blue, Samsonite cases.

We got the call from Abbie who was just checking that everything was OK and he reassured us that travelling separately was the right thing to do.

"With the bags being identical, it doesn't look good going together, you're not a married couple."

I remembered when we received the cases at the market from the drop-off guy. We were in stealth mode, just like the chameleon, blending into its surroundings, then we get given these two Identical brand spanking new cases.
We looked at each and realised that we stuck out like a sore thumb.

Then, just to accentuate our presence we hear:

"RUSSIAN PROSTITIUTES? CAN DO. HAPPY MASSAGE? CAN DO. BOLLYWOOD STAR? CAN DO."

It was bloody Cando.
He'd brought the drop-off guy and was now slowly driving past us with the window down.
I leant in towards his open window.

"I'll tell you what you can't do... shut the fuck up."

Jake announced,

"I have a plan. In the next few days, Soft Mick is coming over from Thailand to do a run somewhere in Europe. Let's send him first, whatcha reckon?"

Soft Mick was 'exactly as it says on the tin'.
A nice fella but a bit on the dense side.
Simple, dopey, ye know the type?
Thick as a brick.

Now, I'm not going to say I didn't have a think about it, or later spent many a long day/night in isolation wishing that I had let him go first, but there was no way I would put anyone on point like that taking one for me.
I wouldn't let anyone do something that I wasn't prepared to do myself.
That would have changed, of course, if I knew what I know now and what Mick was like.

I would later meet him again on one of my first home leaves from a UK prison and that's when I found out that he got arrested in India the same day that I got arrested in Japan, and he'd spent a horrific four years in a Mumbai prison slum.
We both arrived back in Thailand at the same time.
I never even took an extra sleeve of smokes again.
Soft Mick?
No, he smuggled meth to Turkey and got caught and was only released in 2021.
Yep, I know what you're thinking... thick as a brick.

"OK, Jake, lets toss for it."

Jake looked at me, eyebrows raised high, with the knowledge that he'd had all the luck playing poker in Goa.

"Bring it on, ye Bald prick!"

"Heads I win, tails you lose?" I said laughing.
God loves a trier.
We used a good old ten bob coin (50p).

I had a stash of different currencies that I always carried with me, and it came in handy many a time.

"Go on, your call."

"Tails never fails," said Jake.

I flipped the coin high in the air, and as it came spinning back down to land on the back of my hand, it bounced off and fell to the floor, spinning around like a mad ballet dancer on speed.
I stamped on it before any of us could see it.

We both looked at each other with wry smiles.

Then, just before we looked, I thought of Jake and his new family that I'd got to know very well.

It felt like I was staring at him for ages, and he pulled his head back into his neck with a frown.

"What?"

They had an 11-month baby boy and in that split second, I just thought,

oh well, if someone is going to get caught and be away for a year or so then it would better be me.

"Reyt, do me a favour pal. If it does go tits up, make sure you take care of The Silverback, clean straw and somtam daily."

Do you want to know who actually won the coin toss?

Tails...it was density! (sic)

Flowery Twats

I watched a few episodes of Fawlty Towers on the way to Hong Kong. I remember well seeing the word 'twat' on the telly for the first time on a Fawlty Towers episode.

I was really shocked.

So, times change and we grow up.
Some of the more astute of you will have noticed that we use a lot of swearing in the book to keep it real and we try to put you there, in the moment but believe me, in real life I'm way more of a foul-mouthed yob.
Go and watch the second podcast me and Woz did with Shaun Attwood; it's a tricky task to keep it real without every other word being a curse.
We even split words up with a swear word such as

'Absofuckinglutely' or 'Fanfuckingtastic',

and even join swear words together. I give you

'Cuntyfuck' and 'Bollockingbastard.

You could use cuntyfuck when something is difficult,
E.g. 'I was trying to get it off, but it was a reyt cuntyfuck'.

Also, when you are a bit flustered.

'That bollockingbastard thing over there'.
Anywho, back to the drugs smuggling.

The flight's departure was delayed at Mumbai airport and I had to endure that dreaded wait on the plane thinking,

.any minute now the doors will open, and my name will be called out..

'Mr. Steven Beattie could you... '

By the time we got to Hong Kong, we were cutting it fine, so four of us from the flight from India had to get the hurry on to our connecting flight to Tokyo and we just made it.

Thirty minutes into the flight, and my name along with the other three was called out on the speaker.

"Sorry, because of the delay, your bags never made it to this aircraft but don't worry they will be delivered to your hotel ASAP."

Brilliant, I thought.

I mean how lucky is that? And...hmmm.

Maybe I've found a sneaky little way in by accident.
Oh, Abbie will love this one and a nice little drop for me,
I'll make sure Jake books the same flight.

It looked like ours was the last plane to land as the airport felt very quiet, and I was nicely at ease recollecting my previous encounter with Japanese customs.

A quick stroll through, get a hotel, and out to watch the footie.

Liverpool were my team and flying high.

They were playing Chelsea and this could finally be the year they got to the top again.

Oh, how soon things could go downhill for me and The Reds.

The customs officers didn't seem right from the off and this wasn't paranoia. I had nothing to be paranoid about. I only had a small 'man bag' for my passport and tickets, but they were going through everything, really going to town. They did a rigorous body search, making me take my trainers **and** socks off and scanning everything with one of them drug detecting stick things.
I was the last man standing in the whole bloody airport so started to protest in a quite naturally-offended way.

"Mate, I'm not being funny but with the flight being delayed, I've still got to get a hotel and I'm going to miss the football match, what's the problem?"

My mate Nessy had another saying –

'it's all gone Hong Kong (wrong)'. Hmmm, how fitting. They just left me stood there and it felt like they were saying to each other,

'ok, what do we do now? his bag is still in Hong Kong so we're going to have to let him go'.
Paranoia, back again my old friend.

I asked a female flight attendant who was walking by what was going on. She had a little chat with them and then all seemed fine.
They came over and apologised,

"sorry sir, we're just doing our job."

And then I was off to Narita town, a short ten-minute taxi ride to a decent hotel of the driver's choice. The Comfort Hotel.

The entrance was two floors up from the lift. I got in the lift along with a Japanese girl.
She was about 25-years-old, I reckon.

"Hi, how are you?" She asked with an American accent.

"Hi, all good thanks. I've just come from the airport. Hey, do you know a bar around here that will show the soccer?"

"Yeah, there's a sports bar in the little town about five minutes away."

"Oh sound, I'll try and find it."

"Oh, I love your accent, I'll take you if you want?"

"I say, you Japanese girls are bang on," I replied in my best Leslie Phillips accent.
I most likely overdid the accent.

"I'll check in, take a quick shower and meet you in the foyer in, say, 20 minutes?"

She was called Julie, a very pretty and friendly girl, born in Japan then adopted by an American family and brought up in Washington. I couldn't believe I'd kind of cracked off in record time, well done me.

'YES. *Still got it*,' I thought to myself.

The sports bar was just what I was looking for and it had a big TV screen. At the bar, as I ordered the drinks, I noticed there was a smartly-dressed British-looking chap.

"Good evening, sir. I didn't expect to see any bloody foreigners around here."

"Yeah mate, I'm a pilot, just on a stopover," said the Australian man. Australian/English, they all look the same to me.

"Oh right, it's not you that lost my bloody bag, is it? That's why I'm stuck here."

"Haha, not Guilty mate. Hey, where have you come from?

"Mumbai, India"

"Oh bugger, they'll be ripping that bag apart mate, make no mistake, eh."

"Really, why?"

"India is a big drug route mate. I see it all the time."

In an instant, I felt really uneasy and then what he said next shook me to my core.

"Look me in the eyes and tell me you're not carrying drugs."

Although I was in shock of what he just sprung on me, I replied swiftly and confidently, and as I stared him right in his eyes, I drawled back at him.

"I'm not carrying drugs but... are you?"

We both laughed and I walked away thinking,
'what the hell.'
It didn't get any better when I was sat chatting with Julie while watching the footy.
I was telling her about my private investigator job, and she asked if I could help out her friend who was convinced his wife was cheating on him.

"Oh, please help him, he's so worried and a good friend of my family. He's a policeman."

Aaaand there goes my arse. Goodbye arse.

What the bloody hell was going on?
I can do without this. I need to give this girl the brushoff.

"Oh sorry. Like I said, I'm here on holiday to see my sister and most likely getting the train up to Hokkaido as soon as my bag turns up."

It was too late as she was phoning him. I mean...WHAT? I've just been asked to look a pilot in the face and say I'm not carrying drugs and now I've just been handed a phone to speak to a Japanese policeman.

"Moshi Moshi," said the cop.

"Erm... hello, look, I'm really sorry and I don't know what Julie has told you but I'm not working, I'm on holiday... erm... sayonara."

I just laughed at the whole awkwardness of the situation whilst downing a beer and pretending to be engrossed in the football match.
It was a good distraction because my mind was off to the races and was all over the place.

I'd got a Japanese sim card for my phone on the way to the bar, so when I went to the toilet, I made sure the coast was clear and I called Pete.
He just laughed and said,

"you been on the cockin' glue again?"
I cracked up with him.

"Mate, it's not funny, my heads going."

"Well, if she's an undercover copper, get her pissed and give her the 'Finger Pie Test'."
I knew exactly what he was on about.
If I got frisky with her and gave her a finger blast then, well, she can't be on the other side, can she?

"Wait a minute, Pete, she can't drink coz she's on some kind of meds."

"Fucking copper." Replied Pete laughing his bollocks off and then put the phone down... twat.

It did make me feel better saying it all out loud.
There's just no way they would go this far, would they? ....
would they?

Liverpool won and it was time to go.

We sat outside on a bench in front of the hotel just chatting (me waiting for the moment to get fishy fingers).
She showed me all her meds and jeez, there was a lot.
What she told me next made me think there was no way she would make this up as a cover story.

"My birth Mum and Dad here in Japan sexually abused and tortured me from an early age until the authorities saw all the bruising. Then I was put in a home where more abuse happened until the age of ten when I was finally adopted by my amazing American parents, but it left many scars. The physical scars I can deal with, but it's the mental scars that are taking longer to heal. I have fits from the physical head bashing."

She told me more truly horrific things that I'm not going write about. It's hard to imagine people (animals) doing that to a child.
OK, enough on that... I only met her that one night, but she most certainly made an impression on me.

A bird's eye view

I checked out in the morning and informed the desk I would be back to collect my luggage when it arrived.
Then I checked into the hotel opposite and made sure I'd got a room that was overlooking the entrance where my suitcase would be delivered. I figured that if something was up, I just might be able to spot anything out of the ordinary.

I knew it was a long shot but...

I feel a right cunt for even thinking this, but it crossed my mind to come up with some excuses to ask Julie to collect my luggage.

'Could you do me a big favour? I've had to go and meet my sister in Tokyo; is there any chance you could collect my bag when it gets dropped off at the hotel and bring it to the city?'

Now, I don't think for a second that she would have got in any trouble but knowing what I do know about the Japanese system, they most likely would have put the poor girl in the police jail for at least 10 days, so thank God I didn't stoop that low.

"Oh shit. Oh shit. Oh shit."

I'd forgotten my lucky traveling Buddha.
I'd put it on the mirror in last night's room and completely forgotten about it, how could I?
What a dickhead.
I couldn't go back for it, could I?
I'd told the same cock and bull story to the hotel staff when checking out about going to Tokyo.

Oh, sod it,' I thought.
It's just all superstitious nonsense anyway.

I bought a load of food and drink and pulled a chair over to the window to begin my surveillance.
I had the perfect view of the entrance to the hotel and it wasn't that busy, so any kind of movement and I was on them like a hawk. I'd ring the hotel every few hours to see if somehow, I'd missed the drop off.

I was shitting it, and when I rang Abbie and asked if there was another option or a way out, he just put it to me straight.

"Motherfucker, stop panicking. If you really want out, I can get you out by boat to South Korea and get a new passport but my friend, think it through. The case will stay uncollected and eventually they will find the drugs and it will all trace back to you. You will be on Interpol's list and forever. Brother, it's up to you."

I didn't like the sound of that so let's look at the worst case scenario.
 The other guys got two years for four kilos and I've only got two kilos, so by that logic, I should only get one year. I mean, it's not class A, is it?
Oh, and as long as they don't suss the stamp that the Chinaman altered from Nepal to the Maldives, the passport should be fine.
I wouldn't even have to tell anyone back home that I'd been banged up abroad.
I'd make up some bullshit story that I went up in the mountains and joined a Buddhist monastery;
well, that's more believable than saying I got caught smuggling drugs to Japan.

I visualised getting caught and what I'd say, I had it all planned out. Keep it simple so not to build a web of lies, the more lies you tell, the more you have to remember.

So, this would be my story.

'It was my first time. so I'll tell you everything I know. Abbie is from Afghanistan or Turkey; I didn't really know or believe anything he said. It didn't matter because I wouldn't be dealing with him again. It was just one job to get me out of the shit'.

I had to have a word with myself.

'Ok enough. Stop thinking the worst in everything.'

But I knew I had to plan for the worst case scenario.

I had sim cards from England, Austria, Netherlands, Denmark, Nepal, India, Hong Kong, Taiwan, Singapore, Lao, Cambodia, and Australia and God knows how many incriminating messages were in them, so I went for a little walk.

In the subway under the train station, I put all the SIM cards in a coke can and put that in the bin to be retrieved after the pickup.

I rang The Comfort Hotel again but nothing.
I tried once more at 10:30 p.m. and nothing again, so I called it a night, thinking the delivery guys just wouldn't be working this late.

I woke up the next morning and had what was to be my last Hookers Breakfast/ Jewish Breakfast. Call it what you like, coffee and cigarettes.
I called the hotel at bang on 9 a.m.

"Hi, it's me again, Steven Beattie? I'm calling about my suitcase to see if it's been dropped off by Cathay Pacific yet?"

"Oh yes, Mr. Beattie, it actually came last night about 11 p.m."

Oh shit. My heart was racing.
I'd most certainly got back that adrenaline rush that I'd secretly missed.

Well, everything seemed normal on the phone, he didn't sound like he was having to think about what he was saying. Ooohhhh... I had a big sigh of relief,

I really thought I'd suss them out in their voice if they were lying.

"Right. Get your shit together lad," I told myself.

I went through my phone one more time deleting all the evidence bombs in my phone.
I knew there was a good chance the police could retrieve any deleted stuff, so the only problem that I could see, was Pete.

I had him down as G and from what we'd texted each other, I knew I could turn it around and say he was just a friend that knew what was going on and was just giving me advice.
As for Abbie?... Well, he was getting all the blame.

I'd asked him earlier about what any DEA or the likes might know about him, and he said,

"They know what I want them to know, Abbie the Motherfucker from Iran."

"Well, motherfucker, I'm grassing you right up, ye cunt, if I ever get caught."

"No problem, it's to be expected."

I sat there having my fourth Coffee starring at the TV that I'd left on all night.

There was a Japanese guy tied to what looked like a big wooden X-shaped cross, legs spread, and then some tart ran up to him and with all her might kicked him Roberto Carlos-style right in the bollocks.

I just stared in disbelief as to what I'd seen and was left trying to figure out why? The poor bloke was in agony.
Then she did it again.
What the fuck was I watching?
This could well be the last thing I see on the telly, ffs.

I went downstairs and hailed a taxi driver,

"Hi, do you speak English?"

"Yes, how can I help you, sir?"

Good start as a lot of the Japanese I'd met, even in tourist jobs, didn't speak the best English.

"OK, let me explain. I want you to go to The Comfort Hotel and pick my suitcase up from the foyer and bring it to this hotel, yes? I just don't have the time as I'm meeting a work colleague here any minute, is that OK? All clear?"

He repeated it almost word for word and off he went.
I legged it to the lift and up to my viewpoint, perfect.
I watched him enter the building. Not three minutes later, he came back out...

NO SUITCASE... DAMN.

I rang the hotel to ask what the problem was.

"Sorry, sir, but we need your passport, and you need to sign for your bag."

OF COURSE THEY DO, YE TIT.
They wouldn't let just anyone just take the bag.
Hmmm, what now?
Coffee, cigarettes, alcohol. Now, let's have a little think.

There was a convenience shop nearby, so I went and bought four cans of courage. I went for one last reconnaissance trip around the area checking for anything out of the norm.

I made three phone calls.

1. "Hiya, Ja (love). I'm just going to book my flight home; I'll be back in three days. Love you, miss you, and all that bollocks."

"Miss you, love you too and Daadam cry for you to come back, layo layo gai-laow (hurry, hurry, old man)."

2. "OK, I'm going for the suitcase now. If it goes wrong, don't send me any money until I get sentenced because it will ruin my story of you being a motherfucker."

"Salam Alaikum, brother."

3. "Oreyt, pal? Right, I'm outside now, all looks normal so, well, I'll call you back in ten minutes... Look after Wanna for me, mate."

"Shitting it, aren't ye? Ya cockin' soft twat. Haha, see thee in a few days, Damage. I'll have a cold one ready."

Going down

Now, I know you that read this right at the very beginning of the book, but given that you are now complicit with all my smuggling exploits, I wondered how it would read a second time.
Will this paragraph read any differently now that you've made the journey to this point in time with me?

Let's find out.

Bollocks, I'm going for it.

Right, here we go, this could be my last beer and last drag of a cigarette as a free man.
As I look up, it's a clear blue sky and I seriously think about asking for divine intervention.
Kind of weird that I've never believed but yet, here I am, thinking about it. Oh, the hypocrisy.
I've been smelling a rat for the last two days and my paranoia is in overdrive, not helped by the fact that on previous occasions, my gut instinct has been bang on.
I walk into the hotel and take the lift to the reception which is on the second floor.
So far, so good.
I go to the desk and ask the manager for my case.

He's a nice guy, I was speaking to him just the night before.
If this guy is in on it, he's a bloody good actor.
Nah, everything seems fine.
It's the bag, the bag is the point of no return.
Once I put my hands on that bag, I'm all in.

I'd ran this scenario over and over in my head and this was the point where they'd get me.
I figured that as soon as I signed for the bag, they'd all come out from nowhere and arrest me.

He gives me the bag and through gritted teeth and with a clenched arsehole, I signed for it.

Nothing.

I suddenly realised I wasn't breathing, so I gently exhaled and went to take a seat to give the suitcase a casual once over.
The luggage tag from India seemed fine, no evidence of tampering.
This is good, this is good. Starting to feel better now.
I check the lock.
I ask the manager, "scuse, mate?"
No reply, so I ask him again.

"Excuse me mate, where's the key?"
He looks clueless and says he doesn't know.
He's in on nothing.
This is going to work.

I found the keys in the top part of the suitcase where I'd bloody left them.
Half an hour from now I'm going to be giving it the Billy bigtime in Roppongi, the sin city area of Tokyo.
All that worrying and overanalysing things, watching that bloody hotel for two bastard days.
Well, once again I'm coming out on top.

Everything is going to be alright.

I head towards the lift.

I press the button and hear the lift coming down; it shatters the calm of the quiet reception area and that's when I heard the clip clop sound of official shoes coming towards me. These footsteps belonged to more than one person and the pace of them did not seem right.
These footsteps had the sound of purpose and intent.
I looked up at the ever-decreasing numbers of the lift's descent.

"Come on… come on."

The sound of the lift was getting louder as it got closer, as were the footsteps.

I was starting to get really tense.

The lift finally slowed as it reached my floor and the pace of the footsteps quickened.
These feet also wanted to get on the lift.
The lift finally settled with a loud clunking noise and then, in the reflection of the steel door, I saw three men in suits stood right behind me. Uncomfortably close in the classic one in front and two either side behind him.
My heart was now pounding.

The doors open.

The arse starts to fall out from my world.

I still cling to the slight hope that this could be just another coincidence.

They follow me into the lift.

Is this shite as like a coincidence?

I keep up the act until the very end and politely ask,
"Are you going up or down?"
They look at each other and don't know how to respond.

I answered for them.
"I know where you're going, you're following me, and I'm going down."

The escalator doors opened and a surge of about 20 people, some with cameras, came at me like the paparazzi do for some big film star or when they come out of a big court case.

It was just a wall of noise that hit me. I recoiled from the barrage of people shouting, all in Japanese and cameras, insanely clicking trying to get the best shot.

I just let out a slow, "ooohhhh noooooo."

I looked down, took a deep breath, and got ready for whatever was going to happen, all the while in the back of my mind I was in don't panic mode.

I thought to myself,

Right, stay cool. It's gone tits up so just deal with it. You're prepared for this, just stick to the story. Remember, keep it simple.

A plainclothes policeman grabbed my wrist quite strongly as another guy said,

"I'm an interpreter for Narita police station and this is inspector Hashimo-to."

"What is your name?"

"Steven Beattie."

"Is this your suitcase?"

I sighed… "Yep."

"What is in the suitcase?"

I didn't see any point in lying. I wanted to give the impression that I'd bottled it and was willing to be completely cooperative with them. It was the only hand that I had to play.

"My clothes and two kilos of cannabis."

That took them aback a little bit and they started chatting in Japanese.

"Oh? how do you know its cannabis?"

That took me aback a little bit and I wasn't too sure what to say.

I was confident that it was cannabis because I'd seen and heard of the guys taking a cheeky wee bit of it (smugglers tax) just before the pickup after getting through customs.
Mad Scotty and Smix would always bring a little smoke or two back and that's why I knew it wasn't the same smell in the Delhi hotel but of course,

I couldn't know that because this was my first time... wasn't it?

"Well, that's what I was told."

"So, you don't know for sure that it's not anything else? Heroin... Methamphetamine?"

What the hell were they suggesting?

So here I am, pants down, red handed, in a whole world of hurt.
The cheese is just about to slide off my cracker and now I've got the possibility that I might have been fucked over and busted for carrying Ice and looking at doing a shit load of time.

"Don't be ridiculous!"

I said it with an 'I'm shocked; what kind of drugs smuggler do you think I am?" tone about me.

"Did you pack it yourself?"

"No."

I started to think,
right, OK, what are they up to? Are they trying to trip me up?

"So how do you know its cannabis?"

I told myself,
'*Ok, keep it simple. I'm just a dumb drug mule doing a run for the first time.*'

"Well, I just trusted them, I was so desperate."

I was trying not to look at all the cameras but when I did, I could totally imagine it being on the local TV stations back home in England.

BLACKBURN MAN, STEVEN BEATTIE, ARRESTED IN TOKYO FOR DRUG SMUGGLING.

whilst being cuffed and shoved into a van with that look of, 'my life has just collapsed' about me and all the rumours running riot back home about what I'd been up to.
I could just imagine them giving it, 'I bloody knew it', and justifying their 'make it up and add bits on' stories about me.

One thing that hit me was how smelly they all were.
I'm not kidding, they had shit breath and everything.

Turns out my that case had been delivered to the hotel the night before, just after I stopped phoning them asking if it had been delivered.

So, everyone, the detectives, the translator, and all the bloody media had to wait all night and be ready for me to pick the case up. In a way, I was glad I didn't get busted until the morning, because at least it gave me one last night of freedom.

All the while them lot had to sit around all night waiting for me.

"OK, Mr. Beattie, we are going to open up your suitcase and test what is in it. OK?"

I wished I could have said 'NO' and that would be the end of it.

They spread out a large blue tarpaulin on the floor, emptied my pockets, and spread everything out on it. Then they took out all my clothes from the case and went through the lot with a fine toothcomb while two guys dismantled the case.
They asked what this was, showing me a small, white, half the size of a pea object.
I think they thought they'd found some type of drug.
I had no idea until I looked at it closer.

" Oh, it's a bit of a Polo."

"Aaa? What Poro?"

"No, Polo."

"Poro?"

"No, Polo. It's a white mint with a hole in it."

He tilted his head to the side and said,
"Hmmm… Poro."

They still had no idea what I was on about, but they were confident they had me on another charge.
I would have loved to see the look on their faces when they tested the Polo.
Someone definitely got called the Japanese version of a daft twat.

Suddenly, the Magnum PI theme tune filled the room.
It was my phone. It was a very weird feeling hearing it here in this situation. It suddenly filled me with even more regret, almost like it was taunting me giving it,

'See? If you'd stuck with me, you wouldn't be in this shit'.
It brought with it a stark realisation that this was the last bit of my free from reality life.

A different reality was waiting for me, and God only knows for how long.

The translator asked me, "Who is that?"

"Magnum PI," I replied dryly.

I think this was one last stab at humour. I said it in an almost can't be arsed fashion because I knew no one would get it.
I also knew the humour days were over.

"Sorry, say that again?"

They showed me the phone screen with 'no caller ID on it, so I just said,

"I don't know; I guess its Abbie. The guy who set it all up."

"Who? The guy that's going to pick the bag up?"

I could see them thinking, '
great we can get them both'.

"No. The guy that sent me. I have no idea who is picking the bag up, I would've been told where to go after I got the bag."

I'd basically answered his next question and they chatted while a younger guy took the phone away.
I guess he was trying to get any info before it was deleted.
The four cans of beer were having an effect on my bladder by now and I kept asking to go to the toilet but they said,

"wait, wait, this first."

It took a while just to get a sample and then they tested it right in front of me saying,

"Blue is class A, (I'm fucked)
Red is class B." (I'm less fucked)

I was convinced they already knew what it was.
I mean, how did they find it in the first bloody place?
I was beginning to doubt everything, thinking,

'are they messing with my head here or what?'

I didn't even see what they tested which really shit me up because if I'd have seen a lump of dark brown resin being tested then fine, but now?
I really didn't know anymore.

Had Abbie pulled a fast one and secretly got me to smuggle ice?

They turned back towards me with a small test tube.

Fuck's sake, my future is in this glass tube.

They gave it good old shake and held it at arm's length towards me.

The police and press all went silent.

Everyone was waiting for the colour to change...

RED

Relief is something that I never really thought about before. There are different kinds of relief, all benefiting you but on different levels.
The relief I experienced in Okinawa when I got away with it was that my immediate future was all good but here, the relief was that my immediate future wasn't going to be as bad. Obviously, the end results were different but that feeling of a weight being lifted is the same.
In Okinawa, I was given more time to continue my escape from reality but here, my reward was being given less time in a harsh reality.

Just imagine if I had been carrying Ice or heroin all this time. The difference in the length of the sentence would have been huge.

"OK, Mr. Beattie, we'll now go to the police station to finish off the investigations."

They still wouldn't let me go to the hotel toilet and the station was only 10 minutes away but I was about to breach. I was begging them.

"Please, I have to pee or I'm going to wet myself."

Finally, I was escorted to a toilet, but I was still cuffed which was very strange even though I was in agony from wanting to piss.
My brain refused to co-operate,

'naa mate, not in front of him'.

I could imagine the policeman thinking I was up to something, planning a desperate run.
Then... finally, the damn burst. Oh, the joy of a piss.
It was orgasmic.

I looked over to my piss pal.

"All better now."

He gave me a knowing nod.

They took me upstairs to what was basically an office room, cuffed one hand to the chair, and then I went through my whole story for the first time... erm, not story, what actually happened.
This was when I met the inspector Mr. Yuki, who would be dealing with me over the next three months, and the translator, Mr. Hiroshi, an American/Japanese guy who was to befriend me.

"Right, before I say anything, I need a cigarette. They wouldn't let me smoke at the hotel and I'm desperate for a ciggy."

"Sorry, no smoking here."

"What? Well, I'm not saying another word until I have a cigarette. I'm sorry, but I know my rights."

I had no idea what my rights were, but I do watch TV.

"Downstairs you can have one cigarette per day, Monday to Friday. No smoking at weekends but once in the main prison, there is zero smoking. These are your rights. I'm very sorry," said Mr. Hiroshi.

Bugger. This isn't the most ideal situation to quit but... OK,

OK, every cloud and all that. I flicked a switch in my head and jumped at the chance to turn what seemed like a negative into a positive.

"Right then, I'm a non-smoker. let's crack on."

Jackanory time

"I'd been traveling about Asia, fell in love, and wanted to stay in Thailand. I'd been working in Australia, but my visa ran out and I'd injured my neck and back, so I started up the private investigator company. I had a few little accidents and ran out of money. That's when I randomly met Abbie in a bar in Bangkok. We'd been chatting a while and after he heard my hard luck story, he offered me a way out. I thought with it only being a class B, it wouldn't be that bad so… here I am."

Not too far from the truth, just a few bits (about half a book) missing.

"A private investigator?" said Mr. Yuki.

So up until this point, I was under the impression that he couldn't speak or understand any English, but he clearly could. Hearing I too was an investigator made him slip from his little act, or maybe it was just legal procedure, I'm not sure.

"Yes, I was a private investigator in Pattaya."

I then went on to explain it all and they did find it fascinating.I kind of felt a little relieved that it seemed to be going so well. No harsh interrogating, no torture (I know, but my head was in the bin. Too many Japanese war films, I guess), or any of the worst-case scenarios that had been running around my head as I stood there at the hotel while they ripped my suitcase apart.

They kept trying different ways to trip me up.
To whom, where, and how was I to drop the bag off?
It was all very simple.
All I had to do was wait for a phone call from Abbie and proceed from there, until then I had no idea. I gave them just enough info on Abbie.
A gay-looking, Middle Eastern man I'd met in a bar.
Can you imagine them looking through a list of suspects in their files?

"He looks gay."
"You think? "
"Yeah, defo.".

I told them we'd only met twice and that's when we'd sorted everything out.
Like I said earlier, I'd spoken to Abbie about this; he was always under the impression he must be on some kind of DEA list and they most likely had his photo, but Abbie wasn't his real name, and all this was way before any of that photo recognition shit (well, that's what we thought).
Basically, I was telling them what they already knew and if not, it wasn't going to affect Abbie in any way.

This took all day because it all had to be tediously copied out, repeated, and signed.
So, at about 5 p.m., that was it, down the stairs and off to the cells.

The cell

I was taken down to the ground floor where my new life awaited me. There was a row of nine cells that all faced the airport and from there, all the prisoners could watch the planes

leaving, filled with people who were free to do what they please.
Was this cruel design intentional?
Knowing what I know now about the Japanese judicial system, I would say yes. They want to make sure you don't come back.

I was passed on from the police to the jailhouse guards who were surprisingly warm and friendly. Two older guys in their 60s. They must have seen many a broken man or woman go through these doors and I'm sure they knew they weren't dealing with any violent types.
Just remorse-riddled drug mules and that's what I was, a stupid drug mule.

They asked me to strip and then the older grey-haired guard said,

"Sumo time. Ok, do same me. Haha."
He then crouched down, spread his legs, lifted one leg, and slammed it down, then the other.
I wonder if that had ever worked, and suddenly a bag of drugs had just popped out?
Imagine if the Amazon a Go Go lady found out about this. She could have a whole new act.

'Sakura the sexy sumo with Fukashi, the unstoppable fanny frog.'
It really took me back thinking about him trying to make me laugh.
It didn't work, but I did a kind of fake and feeble 'haha' to make him feel appreciated in his effort.

I was led to the first cell, (Bango 1.)
It looked not too dissimilar to an American jailhouse as seen in the films with iron bars about a fist apart.
Another guard, a small odd-looking chap, opened the door and in I went.
I wasn't alone.

There were three other guys in with me who were all sat down and they stood up to greet me saying hi or hello in a very passive and sombre way.
I really had no idea what to expect and to be honest, I'd never even worried about what the other guys would be like.
Two of them looked like they were Japanese.
One was an old frail-looking fella and the other a younger lad of about 30 who looked like an Asian Michael Jackson (The white Michael Jackson), and the last guy was a big, physically fit looking Aussie bloke which I didn't expect.

"Sit down, mate, you'll be ok here. It's just a bit bloody boring, ay?"

"I haven't got to the boring bit yet, but yeah I can imagine, that's not been the day I had planned, I can tell ye, haha. How you doing? I'm Ste from England...I just got busted for two kilos of cannabis."

And then I gave that 'pull yer mouth back into your face with that Wallace and Gromit smile.'

"Aahh, mate ye be right, ay, most of them in here are in for ice and looking at a ten stretch, ay."

Oh, that was better, a bit of positive thinking, I liked this guy right from the off.
They all came across as really friendly, maybe this wasn't going to be that bad after all. A nice warm cell, good mates, and a bit of Britpop playing in the background to boot.

The food being brought out on trays was not the worst looking grub and we had cups of green tea.
Hey, a few more months of this and I'll be able to get myself fit again.
Well... what can I say?
Lesson learnt.

Nightmare in Narita

> It would give me great pleasure to hear that you have freed yourself from the slavery of the weed. Please sign the letter and add your comments, and send it back to:
> Allen Carr, The Easy Way to Stop Smoking,
> 1c Amity Grove, London SW20 0TW
>
> ----
>
> Dear Allen,
> YIPPEE! I'M A NON-SMOKER
> Signed STEVEN BEATTIE   Date 23 10 08
> Name NARRITA TOKYO PRISON
> Address _____
>   Postcode H·E·L·L

    The cell was exactly eight by eighteen steps in size (yep, I measured it out).
At the back of the cell and to the right was a cubicle which was the toilet. It had a metal door to give you a bit of privacy, however, the part of the cubicle that faced out towards the door of the cell was made of glass.
There was a metal panel which went up to your waist to give you a bit of dignity when you were sending a sausage to the seaside but it was not ideal for those who are of a nervous disposition when it comes to dropping one off.

The idea was that they could see if anything untoward was going on. I don't mean men on men untowardness, I mean suicide. The longer I stayed there, the more I realised how necessary it was.
Suicide attempts were common here.

There was a big steel meshed window just to the left of the toilet. That was the view to the outside world and looked directly onto the airport... nice.
In between the mesh window and the actual exterior window was a walkway where the guards patrolled every ten minutes.

Kenny was the older guy in the cell. He was 59 years old but looked older, was very frail, and seemed permanently cold. I just hoped that it wasn't a direct result from being in here. He couldn't speak much English and had the look of a man who had lived a life and had seen and heard more than enough of everybody's shit.
He didn't really need to speak, he had this ability to just give you a nod. If you didn't know what the nod meant, then there was no point in telling you.
Kenny was from Narita and was in for some big insurance fraud.

Wacko, as I called him, was the younger lad and couldn't speak a word of the Queen's, he just did bits of exercise and read the comic books that were provided.
Turned out he was Chinese and working without a visa, so was just being deported.
I wished that was me.

Simon was an Australian pilot (that was two that I'd met in three days) who also lived in Narita.
He was married to a Japanese woman and had kids.

He was in here for getting into a fight in a pub.

A Yakuza guy was being a bully and getting heavy with the other customers so Simon, being a big strapping 6'2 fella, stepped in to help. All hell broke loose and inevitably the police arrived and somehow, he got the blame.
Well, that was his story.
After ten days in here he would end up with a fine, but it looked like it would cost him his job.

So, we all had a little story, and I would gladly swap mine with any of them.

Food came on a tray delivered through a trap at the bottom of the door. A schnitzel-type thing with rice and pickled veg, it wasn't the best but at this point food was just a functionality.
It was as though I was completely separated from my body. Almost like a third-person point of view.
My inner self was in complete denial. Refusing to engage in the reality that I was in. Everything around me was just happening and my body went along with it.
I was constantly waiting to wake up.
We've all had dreams where we wake up from a terrible nightmare and you just lay there with all the emotions running through you and then you realise it was just a dream...

it wasn't real...

'Oh, thank fuck for that'.

I'd turn to Wanna and wake her up to tell her,
    "Wow, Wanna, I just had the maddest of dreams, I was in a Japanese prison, it was so real".
She would fart and ask me to go get som tam, and I would go get a coffee and mull over the mad dream I just had.

'Wow, imagine if that was real?'
It is real.

I'm here.

Up to my neck and it's getting deeper.

Every night at 8:30 p.m., each cell would randomly be chosen to wash themselves and brush their teeth.
The Japs don't like you getting into a routine such as cell one first, then cell two for example.
That way, plans can be formed so mixing everything up every day keeps you guessing and on the back foot.
There were four wash basins and they were right in front of our cell, so I would get to see the rest of the inmates when they came to wash.

There was a good mixture of people, mainly Asian but a good dollop of them were from all around the world.

When your cell was called up, a tray was waiting for you with your toothbrush, toothpaste, and soap on it, as well as a small hand towel.
With your ablutions completed, we would then go to a room to collect our bedding.

Our bedding was just a futon, a quilt, and a grubby-looking pillow. Then, we would all return to our cells and ten minutes later, the lights would be dimmed.
Oh, I forgot to mention.

So, about thirty minutes prior to all this, the guards would come round and pass out the allocated sleeping tablets.
That way, by the time you had cleared your cell, washed up, and sorted your bed for the night, the pills would kick in and it was off to the land of nod.
The whole place soon turned into a snore-fest.

I, on the other hand, didn't sleep a wink.
This would be the beginning to a series of the longest nights imaginable or do I mean unimaginable?

We laid our futons out which was basically just a thin mattress, and we were given a grubby quilt which wasn't too bad as long as the heating was on.
Well, it could be worse,
I've definitely slept in worse situations.

Everyone seemed to quickly drift off to sleep but I just laid there going over and over the day's events doing the classic, should have, would have, could have scenarios and became deeply concerned for Wanna and what she might do once she eventually found out what had happened to me.
I left that concern for another day hoping that Pete hadn't told her yet because there have been one or two incidents in the past when for one reason or another -no sim, Wi-Fi down etc., that the carrier didn't get in touch for a day or so.

What the hell was going to happen to me over the next few days… weeks… even years? God only knew.

I don't want to sound like Mr. Tough Guy, but I had no fear of the police or the other inmates. In fact, most of them were just poor sods that had fallen on bad days.
Going to Fuchu, which was the main prison, and dealing with the Yakuza, was intriguing to me.

Ye see, in general, I'm a happy go lucky type and not overtly aggressive, but I can deal with violence accordingly.

I just lay there, going through the many scenarios that could come my way.

At 7:30 a.m., the lights came back up and we gathered our futons and took them back to the storeroom.

Then it was a quick wash and clean your teeth and back to cell.

We took a bucket, brush, and towels in with us to clean the cell and the toilet.

Simon was a great help in those first two days before he was released and helped me so much in such a short time.
He taught me basic Japanese; numbers, greetings, and a rough idea of the procedure and the time scale.
Judging by what all the other inmates had gone through, I would say that on average it took two to six months to get sentenced.

Once sentenced, I would then be sent to a detention centre called Chiba to be processed and then off to the main prison, Fuchu.
Like everyone else, he knew very little about Chiba and Fuchu, only that they were extremely strict, not like here.

The Embassy

A guard came to the door, my name was called, and I was hand-cuffed and off I went up the stairs again.
I presumed that it was for more questioning but no, this was to be a different experience.
On my way up, I could hear this hysterical screaming echoing through the building.
It really put the fear into me,

'*what the fuck are they doing to her?*'

As I was led down the corridor, I went past the room that she was being held in and she just kept on screaming the same phrase over and over again. I'm pretty sure she was South American, but whatever they were doing to her or whatever they had just told her wasn't good.

I tried to put a positive twist on it thinking,

'*See? I'm not having it too bad. Could be a lot worse*'.

Then I started down the line of thinking that maybe this is the next phase.

Maybe, It was like 'good cop, bad cop' and I was off to get some bad cop treatment and end up like her.

I was taken to a very bright, sterile room at the end of the corridor which just had a table and two plastic chairs either side.

I was seated and they cuffed me to the table which was secured to the floor.

They just left me sat there, alone with every possibility of what was going to happen next going through my head.

I heard the door open behind me and could hear footsteps walking towards me.

I braced myself for the worst.

"Well, that's an awful hullabaloo out there, isn't it? Well, not to worry, the cavalry's here."

The instantly reassuring voice sat down in front of me.
Sat opposite me was a young Captain Ashwood from the classic British series, It Ain't Half Hot Mum.
Enter Henry Poppycock.

You might be surprised to read that's not his real name which I can't divulge here but I thought it would give you a good mental image of my great British hope.

"Hi Steven, I'm Henry Poppycock, one of the consular staff for the British Embassy. I'm here to help you as best as I can but here in Japan, there's very little we can do to be honest."

OK, not the best start, but he seemed like a good lad and keen to help out best as he could.

"Nice one, mate, I do appreciate it. I'm still in a bit of shock to be honest. Could you make some phone calls for me, I don't know how all this works, can you put me in the picture please?"

"Right... well, we have a solicitor on the way for you unless you can get a private one? We can also help with that."

"Oh great, and no, I'll take the freebie, thanks, I have no money."

It was all going fairly well; I almost expected him to say, 'Hey, in a couple of months or so we'll get you transferred back to the UK and released.'

What he did say haunts me to this day.

"I'm sorry to tell you, Steven, you've been arrested for smuggling cannabis at the worst of times. You see, there have been a couple of big news stories recently. Students from the top university in Tokyo and a famous sports star have been caught smoking the old 'Mary-Jane' and the government now want to have a big crackdown and make examples of anyone caught with it."

'Oh, that's just frigging brilliant,' I thought and then his next words just snatched the life right out of me and literally knocked me back in the chair.

"You're looking at four to ten years."

I reeled back and just stared at him.

I couldn't hear or feel anything,

I was just stuck in this empty void.

I'm not sure how long it was before I could respond...

"But... you don't know how much I was carrying, do you?"

I was racking my brain searching for a reason as to why he must be mistaken.
He just stared back at me.
He didn't have to say anything.
The look said everything.

"But... it's... it's only two kilos."

"It doesn't matter how much you were carrying. They're cracking down on drug smuggling and you're to be made an example of."

I went on to tell him about the two guys that got two years for twice as much as me.

"So by that reckoning, I should only... oh, what's the point. I'm fucked, aren't I?"

"I'm really sorry, Steven but that was then. I'm just going off what I've been told at head office."

I wouldn't have it and kept up my internal optimism.

'*He must be wrong, he's only young, he must be getting mixed up with class As or something, he must be wrong, no way... up to ten years? NO WAY... he must be wrong.*'

"Can I get transferred soon?" I pleaded.

"We're already on with that but it will take a while. I've only been here six months so it's still very new to me and we don't have many British here. I can't give you any details, I'm sorry, but as soon as I know, you'll know. If not through me then another member of the embassy and we'll come to see you every three months for an hour's chat to see how you're doing."

"OK. Well, thank you and..."

I didn't know what to say.
I had loads of questions planned but they all fucked off as soon as they heard the bad news.
He gave me the address for the Embassy and told me other things that went straight in one ear and out the other...

'... four to ten years... he must have it wrong?'

I went back down to my cell and just sat down, put my head in my hands, and silently wept.
The others didn't say anything. They knew it wasn't good, so they gave me time to come to terms with it and would let me decide whether or not to tell them in my own good time.
It's incredible how fast a bond can be formed in such a short time trapped in a box. Although, I don't think there is a short time trapped in a box.

I sat there just going over it, he must have it wrong.
He's only young and brand new at the job.
Maybe he was thinking it would somehow be better to exaggerate the length of the sentence so that getting two years

wouldn't seem that bad?
I was clutching at straws here, but in the past, I've always found a way out of a bad situation, either by luck or design.

I decided to share the news with my cell mates but before I did, I had to compose myself.
There was no way I could explain the situation without getting my head together first. Also, I had the slight problem of saying it out loud.
To me, at that place in time, I was in the mindset of, if I say it out loud it makes it true, and I really didn't want this to be true.
Denial?
Of course it is, but when your world goes tits up then so does your thinking.
I strapped on my man pants and faced the truth.
 I told the lads,

"I've just met the British embassy guy and he thinks I'm looking at four to ten years."
I wanted them to protest and laugh at how wrong he was and reassure me that I was right saying something like,

'Nah, one, maybe two at the most. you'll be transferred back to civilisation after a few months.'
Collectively, they all did their version of,

'Oooh… bugger'.

I went on to explain how young and inexperienced he was and that maybe he was overdoing it a bit for my benefit.
I looked around at them to cling on to any hopeful words of agreement but, no.
Simon did his best.

"At least it's not ice, mate, like most of these poor sods, ay? It could have been a lot worse, mate."
Simon was right and I desperately tried to cling onto what he said to stop me thinking about those horrendous four words.

'Up to ten years.'

Sticks and stones

After another very plain lunch, I went back upstairs to continue the investigation. I was offered a hot black coffee which I gratefully accepted. I could feel the withdrawal symptoms from the caffeine and cigarettes taking their toll. I wasn't too bad with the alcohol. In fact, of all the things I longed for, I never once thought about a drink.

So come on then, let's get on with it.
I've got it all planned out and ready. I may be well out of my comfort zone here but I'm mentally strong enough to take whatever you've got.

Let's have it.

"What is your father's name?"

I couldn't respond.

I just put my head down to my hands as I couldn't fully lift my hands up to my face because I was cuffed to the chair.

This came out of nowhere and hit me like a ton of bricks.
Mr. Yuki, without realising it, had broken me straight away with one very simple question.
This was the first realisation of what I'd done to my name, my family name.

It really knocked me for six.

It was only now that it hit me that I was the baby boy of the family, and had four sisters and one brother that would be worried sick about me.

'Oh, shit what have I done,' I thought.

Both Mr. Yuki and Mr. Hiroshi were taken aback by my sudden breakdown of sorts and now they didn't know how to respond.
Mr. Hiroshi was cool and said,

"it's ok, take your time, we're in no rush. We understand how emotional things can get."

"Let's have another coffee break," said Mr. Yuki

I hadn't finished my first coffee, but I appreciated the sentiment. Overall, the investigation was still going ok.
They seemed to fixate on all the wrong things.

I had a $1 note that I got from Mumbai airport when I bought a sleeve of cigarettes and, oddly enough, I had to change rupees to dollars. $19 for a sleeve, so $1 change, but it's like they didn't believe me.
I mean, all they had to do was ring the airport up and it would be confirmed, but no.

Hours of going over it all, translated and copied out, repeated and signed.
I really didn't mind because there was a better view from the office window.

One time when they both went out, I blew at the file of papers on the table in front of me for a bit of a cheeky peek and I saw two things of interest.

One was a map of the hotel in Santa Cruz and the other was a map of the car park area outside of The Comfort Hotel where I got arrested.
I noticed what looked like markings of where I'd been staking out the place.
So, they had been onto me.
They had been watching me, trying to watch out for them kinda thing.

See?

Bet you all thought I was paranoid as fuck, didn't you, with all my surveillance and stuff?
The good old Spidey sense always keeps me out of trouble. Well...nearly.

I still didn't know how long they'd been onto me.
I did ask them if they knew I was coming or had been tipped off in any way and also if Lisa was any part of it but they said, and not very convincingly,

"No."

They also wanted to know every detail of all the cards in my wallet.

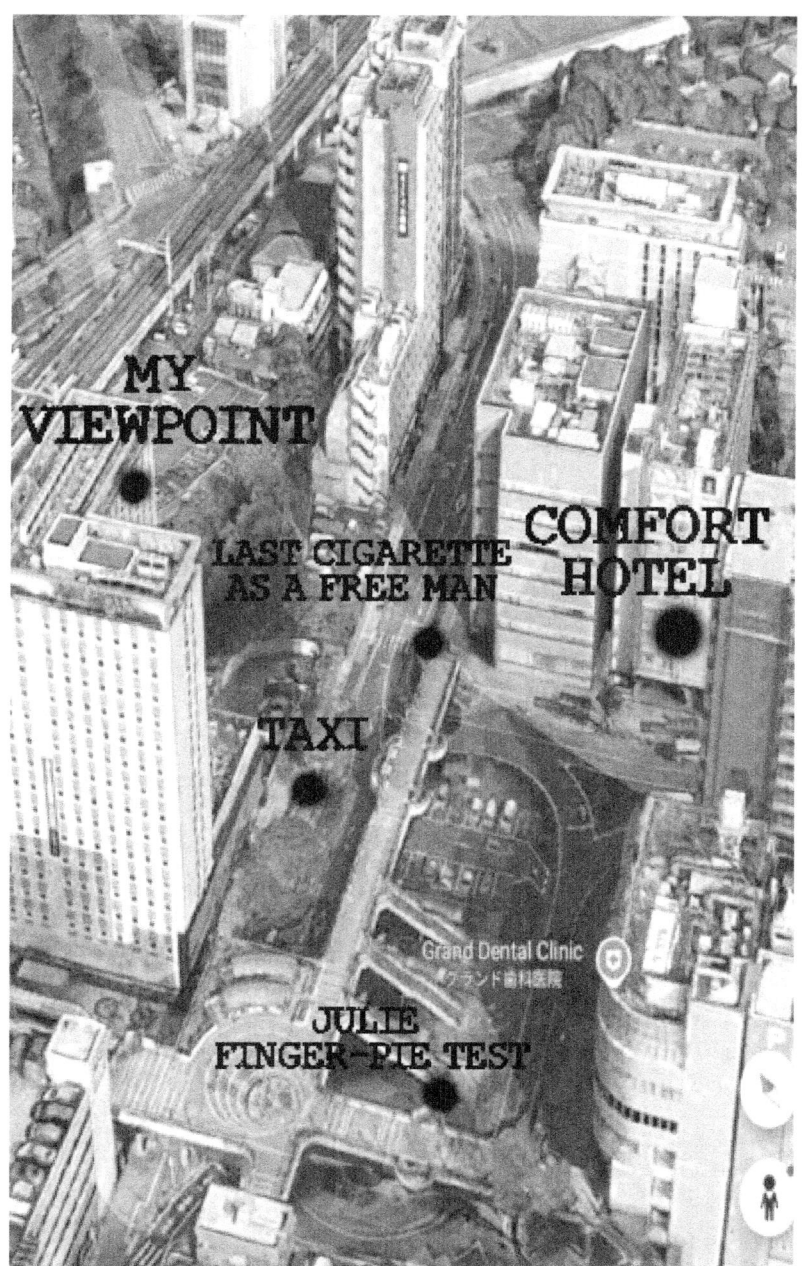

Chiba

On the third day, I was told I'd be taken to see the prosecutor in Chiba, a place I'd never heard of until Simon put me in the picture two days previously and I only wish it had stayed like that.
I was again cuffed and then roped together with two others, Kim and a very quiet man whose name I never got to know. He didn't speak much but you knew he was in big trouble, as was Kim.

He'd been in the same cell at Narita for 8 months on a conspiracy charge; I'd only been in there for three days and that was hard enough to get my head around.

Just getting outside, regardless of where I was going or what would happen to me, was a great relief.
Oh, to get that tiny bit of fresh air and to see real life going by was a joy to behold, and this was after only three days.

Looking out through the tinted windows, I could see that some Halloween decorations had gone up.
Just watching people walking about, free to go where they like and do what they want to do and here am I, cuffed on a 50-minute minibus ride to courts of some sort.

Kim warned me it would be a long day and I'd get interrogated for maybe an hour or so.

"Interviewed, you mean?"

I was thinking maybe he's got mixed up with his English although it was pretty good to be fair.

He shook his head wishing he had got it wrong and then nodded repeating the word.

'interrogated'.

'Oh shit,'.
He stared right into me,

"hitojichi shiho"

"a what?" I could barely hear him he said it so quietly.

"hitojichi shiho…the hostage system."

I could see him realise who he was talking to.

"of course you don't know about it, the people out there don't know about it."

"No mate, to be honest I know very little about Japan other than Karaoke, sushi and old war movies"

He nodded with a wry smile acknowledging my feeble joke and then with a sigh went on to explain what the hostage system was.

"Once you are arrested then that is it, you are guilty. They don't see it any other way. They are so confident that you have committed the crime they will resort to any means to get your confession. The torture can go on for twelve hours a day and they can hold you for as long they want until you confess."

"They'll torture you? What, physically torture you?"

He looked down at the floor, then slowly raised his head to meet my eyes and tapping the side of his forehead he re-plied,

" no."

I just stared back at him. I knew what he meant and ordinari-ly I would have probed him for more information, but he put the shits right up me.

I was morbidly curious, but I could clearly see that he didn't want to go into it.

"what the fuck have I got myself into?"

Once we got to Chiba I tried to prepare myself for what was to come. My conversation with Kim had given me a pretty good heads up.
Right.
OK then, hmmm.
Maybe now's the time for the bad cop routine.

'Just keep to the bloody story', I repeated in my head.

We were then crammed into a cell about the same size as Narita but with 20 or so stinking bodies, it was hell.
The fluorescent lights were so bright and they had a weird effect on me and were sketching me out.
Oh jeez, just standing in one spot was torture.

If you can, imagine standing in a packed lift with all the awkwardness of accidently leaning into each other and trying to keep within your own boundaries.
Well imagine doing that for ten hours.

I spent most of the time with my eyes closed just trying to zone out everything about this cell and would pass the time trying to pass the weight from one leg and then later on to the other and then equally onto both legs without actually moving. I couldn't wait to get interrogated, as mad as that sounds.

Kim said they had five prosecutors who were all very determined to win and get to the truth, especially a small bald guy with thick round glasses.

So eventually, when I was called, I was faced with a nice looking, respectable, middle-aged woman.

That was a relief.
You know the old saying,
"never judge a book by its cover"?

Yeah.

The iron lady of Chiba

Yep, picture a Japanese Margaret Thatcher with a hangover and a stutter, who could see right through to the lying little git that I was.
Luckily, because I had to have a translator it created a delay between questions and answers and you kinda breakup their rhythm, which then dulls their intensity and gives you time to evaluate your answers. That and plenty of,

"ha?... eh?...what?"

Thankfully, they persisted in barking up the wrong trees.

"Why did you go to Hong Kong so many Times?" said Maggie via her translator.

"Just to do my visa, it's a reyt piss about, and I have to leave Thailand every month to get it sorted".

The translator looked very confused, they leaned into each and there was a bit of back and forth and then the translator asked,

"what is a reyt a piss about?"

Hearing a Japanese girl trying to do a Lancashire accent was something to behold.

I chuckled and replied.

"You know?... A pain in the arse."
Another puzzled look and again they did that University challenge conferring thing.
I realised what I'd said and where I was, so I interrupted them in my best Queens,

"It was rather a palaver."

We all just stared at each other, gormless.

The translator broke the stupor.

"Shall we move on?"

They scoured my passport to check that the dates matched my answers.

"Why did you go to Australia so many times?"

I was quite happy to answer all these questions and it took the most part of that first day.
I had to disguise the fact that I was shitting it as they went through my passport right in front of me, and was desperately hoping they didn't suddenly say,

"What about this?"
and point to the altered Maldives stamp.
That would be all they needed to suss that this was most definitely not my first time, and if they pulled on this loose thread, it would unravel my tapestry of deceit and could quite possibly add another two years to my sentence just for the forgery alone.

Then, she showed me a business card that she'd pulled from my wallet.

"What is this?"

She let me have a good look.
I honestly had no idea.
I had loads of cards in my wallet and most of them I probably got when I was pissed.

"I'm really sorry but I don't remember getting it, I guess I just swapped cards with someone in a bar maybe?"

They asked lots of different questions but kept going back to that card, which I found odd.
For them it seemed really important but to me it meant nothing.

"So, this card, L.K. Metro. Do you know this address?"

L.K. Metro is now a buzzing new Soi full of everything a tourist would want and is very much the heart of Pattaya but back then it was just a couple of bars and a Go Go's with a few shops knocking about.
I didn't have the foggiest idea about this address.

"Why would you have this card but know nothing about it? Why are you lying about this? What have you got to hide?"

Hide? I was really puzzled as I stared at the card and the name Kenneth Horsfield....hmm...I couldn't place it at all.

I even tried to attach a nickname to the name to jog my memory.
Horse?
Horsey?
Fuck knows.
All I knew was this seemed to be important to her and therefore, it would be important for me to know why.

All the while I was going through this internal dialogue, I could feel the glare from this bitch of a woman trying to stare into my soul for the truth.
I mean it does look strange to have a card in your wallet and then to say.
"I don't know anything about it."
If the shoe was on the other foot, I'd think I was lying.

"But you are lying! " I hear you say.

Yeah, but not about the card.
she doesn't know that.
Well...she kind of does but she can't prove it.
Only we know for sure.
You and I, dear reader.

With this constant barrage of questions about a card that I knew buggar all about I started to feel a bit guilty.
I wouldn't have been too confident on passing a lie detector test over this bastarding card!
There was a very uneasy atmosphere, but I was quite happy with how it was going because it **was** the truth.
I didn't know anything about the card.
My sob story of being a first-time drug mule,
"it was him, Abbie did it …. The Middle Eastern guy from Bangkok"

wasn't being questioned at all.
I asked her.

"Why are you so fixated on this card?
The translator seemed hesitant to ask her, even though she bloody well understood every word that I said.
She didn't say a word and just stared at me as though we were in a poker game and she was trying to figure out if I was bluffing or not.

After what seemed an eternity of us just staring awkwardly back at each other suddenly, she stood up and in perfect English said,

"GO! Next time tell me the truth about the card or you'll be staying here a very long time."

Back in the cell, it felt even more claustrophobic than the morning.
The cell was filled with mostly Japanese detainees, and there was just a wall of noise from all the intense conversations.
I presumed they were all telling each other how hard done by they were, and how they were innocent.
At least I got my back to the wall which in itself was a win after the long morning of just being stood upright with my eyes closed, solely concentrating on not freaking out.

(As I'm writing this, I've had a cold shudder re-living the events and I'm right back there. That memory will always be with me. I lean back on my comfy chair just shaking my head. Oh, the relief.)

We were given some food. It was not the best and was delivered through a hatch in the door with a cup of very weak green tea.

It broke the day up, but it didn't shut them up, in fact it sounded worse.

The Japanese language when spoken aggressively is very staccato sounding. So, in a crowded prison cell with everyone trying to be heard over everyone else it was almost like a snare drum being rat-a-tatted over and over again with me almost blinking and wincing on every beat.

As the seconds, minutes and hours went by, the mind games with Maggie in comparison, didn't seem that bad at all.

We were steadily filtered out one at a time and were sent back to whichever police station, detention centre, or Prison that we'd come from.
It was so frustrating and way worse than the cell in Narita.
It did become more bearable as the cell emptied and then finally my name got called.

"Oh… thank god!"

I could never imagine that I'd feel any joy about being cuffed and roped to five other men.
This was only my first trip out and already I dreaded the thought of going back in there.
It's hard to believe that in just a few months' time I'd look back at that place as a Nirvana.

On the bus ride back, I soaked up the everyday goings on out in the free world.
Embracing the views through the bus window which had now become like a portal to a very different world to mine.

I vividly recall seeing an American-style Steak House with the big horns in flashing reds lights and slavering at the thought of eating there.
I thought back to when I was tucking into two big T bones as

Wanna ate Somtam in the street, which shifted my thought to her.

oh dear,

I hope she's OK.

Meet The Gang

Back in Narita, before we went to our cell, we were taken to a holding room and given a late meal of some type of meat and rice.
Me and Kim had a chat about the day's events.
Kim was about 60 years old and a big guy. He had been around and his wisdom commanded respect. When he spoke, his voice had a very calming effect, and he instantly put you at ease. He was looking at spending the rest of his life in prison and for a man who was in so much shite, it amazed me that he was still concerned for my wellbeing.
Basically, the prosecutors wanted him to inform on his fellow Yakuza but there was no chance of him doing that.
He told that me his firm, The Yamaguchi, would execute his family if he spoke a word against them.
He obviously couldn't tell the prosecutors about his dilemma, so they thought he was just being a stubborn old bastard and were basically mentally torturing him in order to break him.
Sadly, this was to be a pattern I'd get to know oh too well.

We were returned to our cells, and I shared what I had gone through with my cellmates.
At the back of the cell, we could communicate with others and three cells down from ours,
I would meet someone who would become a friend for life.

Pier

Pier was an architect who was born in Cameroon but brought up in Belgium and was living in London at the time of his arrest.

He was a softly spoken man who spoke excellent English and was well-educated and very artistic; his drawings were second to none.

He didn't drink, smoke, and would never be involved in any shady activities whatsoever.

His wife was due to give birth to their first child just before Christmas. He arrived at Narita the same day as me after spending five days in a hospital shitting out a kilo of meth pellets that he'd swallowed.

'So, Ste, how the bloody hell did that happen?' I hear you say.

Well...

He was a successful architect and was given the chance to become part of a lucrative company in Los Angeles. Even though it would cost him his savings to set the whole thing up, it was a huge opportunity to give his family everything they had ever dreamed of and make the family proud.

His parents back in Cameroon were poor but had saved and given everything for Pier's education in Belgium so that he could make something of himself and drag the family out of poverty.

Pier had done this and wanted to do more.

He'd met a couple of businessmen while working in Dubai and seeing how they all came from the same part of the world, they got on well.

They had some serious connections in real estate in a very affluent area of California, so Pier put all his eggs into one basket and after a couple of months in the states trying to make this new business work, it fell through and he lost everything.
He didn't even have the money for a return ticket back to the UK.
Thankfully, his Nigerian business partners had a way to help out a friend in need.

That was lucky, wasn't it?
Yep, he'd been conned.

The whole thing was an elaborate plan to get his money and then help him get the money back by giving him the 'choice' to smuggle drugs into Japan.
Having lost everything and with no way of getting back to his pregnant wife, all he had to do was swallow a few packets of drugs, deliver them to Tokyo, and that was it, £5,000 and a ticket home.
He could then rebuild his life and put this down as a lesson learned.

As soon as he arrived in Narita airport, he didn't feel right, like maybe one of the packets had leaked and when a customs officer asked if he was OK, he sat down on the floor and told them,

"No. I'm really sorry but I think I'm going to die. I've swallowed something, I don't know."

He just wanted to get a message back to his wife and family to say how stupid and sorry he was before he faced the true judgment of his God.

They took him to a nearby hospital straightaway and flushed him of the drugs and he made a full recovery.
Fucking dodgy Nigerians.

He felt so stupid and naïve to fall for a scam like that. People will always say,

'you'll never get me falling for something like that,'
but there's a reason why they keep pulling these scams. They work.

We got on really well chatting away at the back of our cells, I think he was drawn to my positive outlook in such a grim setting and our love of art also connected us.
He would be the first person I'd call out to for help if I felt the negativity creeping up on me.

"Pier, you fancy a quiz?"

"Yes, Steven, ... hmm... geography, no? Ten questions, see you in 30 minutes."

We'd then sit down and rack our brains thinking of good and interesting questions about the world or whatever topic we chose.

"Gee, are you in?"

"Yeah, buddy, and this time, I'm gonna kick both your arses haha."

Gee

Gee was only 26 years old and had come from his home city Vancouver with another young lad called Tim on a snowboarding adventure but, on arriving in Narita the customs found three kilos of meth in each of their badly-designed suitcases.
Gee had no idea what the hell had happened.

A friend of theirs (their version of Abbie) had organised the trip and Gee thought they must have been set up.
The other lad, Tim (who I would meet later in Fuchu), had been separated from Gee and on the first day of questioning (interrogations), had cracked and went for the 'I'll tell you everything you want to know' approach.
The problem was he really did tell them everything they wanted to know, dropping Gee right in the shit, as all three of them had planned the whole trip together.

Gee stuck to his story and pleaded his innocence all the way through, adding that Tim and the other guy must have set him up. None of their plans worked as they were both found guilty of smuggling three kilos of crystal meth and each got 10 years' hard labour.

I got to know both lads and they were sound as a pound with not one bit of bad in them, and to think that they were in their primetime years of their lives is a hard one.
Imagine losing that period in your life between the ages of 26 and 36.
Look back at what you did in those years when you were at your fittest and best.
That was gone for these lads.
Well, if you do the crime then...BOLLOCKS...the law needs changing.

Keeny

Now, we talked a little bit about Keeny earlier.
He was in there all the way through my 99 days in Narita and became my Sensei and would help me through my introduction to prison life in Japan.

He had never been to Thailand but had a Thai wife and told me that although his name was actually Kenny, his wife would call him Keeny which meant handsome.

I laughed and told him that keeny was short for the word 'keenyow' which translates as 'mean'.
He let out a knowing chuckle, nodded his head, and I could see that he was missing her.
I laughed with him as I realised how much I missed the Thai sense of humour.

Keeny left a lasting impression on me and his ability to deal with idiots and not entertain bullshit would become part of me and saved many a moron from getting a good thumping.

JP

'Wacko', my Chinese cellmate, was extradited back home after five days, and he was to be replaced with J.P.
I can't remember his real name because after only a few hours listening to him retch and spit, I called him JP (Japanese Pig). I do apologise if I've offended any pigs by way of my blatant speciesism but hey, what can I do?

He'd just come in from holidaying in Koh Samui Thailand, and tried to bring back just a bit of Thai weed for personal use.
He ended up just (when I say 'just', he actually lost a lot for what he did) having to pay a fine but he also lost his job teaching computer studies at a school because the media got hold of it and the story got into the papers which sealed the deal, so when I say 'he just got a fine', it was actually a hell of a lot more than that.
It was a life changer just for a bit of weed.

He absolutely drove me crackers with the constant clearing of his throat. It seemed like every few seconds, he would just make that horrible retching sound and he would be constantly talking utter shite to poor Keeny who would just politely nod at his drivel.

I felt partly responsible for Keeny's torture because JP was telling me how he could no longer go back to Thailand because he was banned for life and he was a typical old perv who could only ever get laid in Thailand. So when I suggested to him that he could always go to the Philippines as it is very similar to Thailand, you could see him come alive inside thinking that his old perv lifestyle could continue.

"Aahh... Phhhiiilipiiiines."

He became a Japanese version of Yoda from Star Wars and would then latch on to poor Keeny telling him all about how he could go to the,
'Phhhhiiilipines'.
He drove us all mental.
I could actually, almost understand what he was saying to Keeny and could predict when he was going to say 'Phhhiiilipines'.

The added torture that people don't take into consideration when they think of being banged up is having to share such a confined place with an absolute prick.
You can't twat them, you can't walk away, you just have to endure.

He was so rude in everything he did with zero thought for anyone else. When stuck in such a small environment, the slightest of things can wind you up.

In some ways, you're looking for a way to vent your own frustrations onto others to release the ever-building tension. I'd exercise as much as I could to get fit to pass the time and give my head a rest. Exercise is the best thing for clearing the head and getting rid of stress and anxiety. There really isn't anything better, well, maybe yoga, but I'd not found that way yet.

I also paced up and down the cell counting each turn around as I'd seen Henry Cherie/Stevie McQueen do in the movie Papillion, but this drove J.P nuts.
He called me the 'crazy bear' like the ones you see caged in zoos.
I could totally understand that it was annoying him and I wasn't trying to bug him, it was just my way of getting through this ordeal.

Most of the time, I would pace up and down purely for exercise but there were a few occasions where I was losing it a bit and I'd pace frantically.
This was actually good for me as it would become a kind of reset where I would reach breaking point, go a bit mental, and then I was good to go until the next time.

I spent 44 days and nights with this arsehole, and it was a good day when he was released.
It was like the cell itself sighed and said,

'thank fuck for that'.

I remember showing Keeny a caricature drawing I had done of J.P. which was a pig's head on a man's body with a meat hook through his head and a speech bubble saying,

'Phhhiiiilipines'.

This hit home and hard with Keeny and he let out a big laugh then abruptly stopped and said quietly,

"You haven't drawn one of me, have you?"

"No, I wouldn't do that to you mate."

Then I pulled out my pencil and pad, stuck my tongue out, and pretended to start drawing him.

Later that day, just before we would get our bedding, we got our new cell mate.

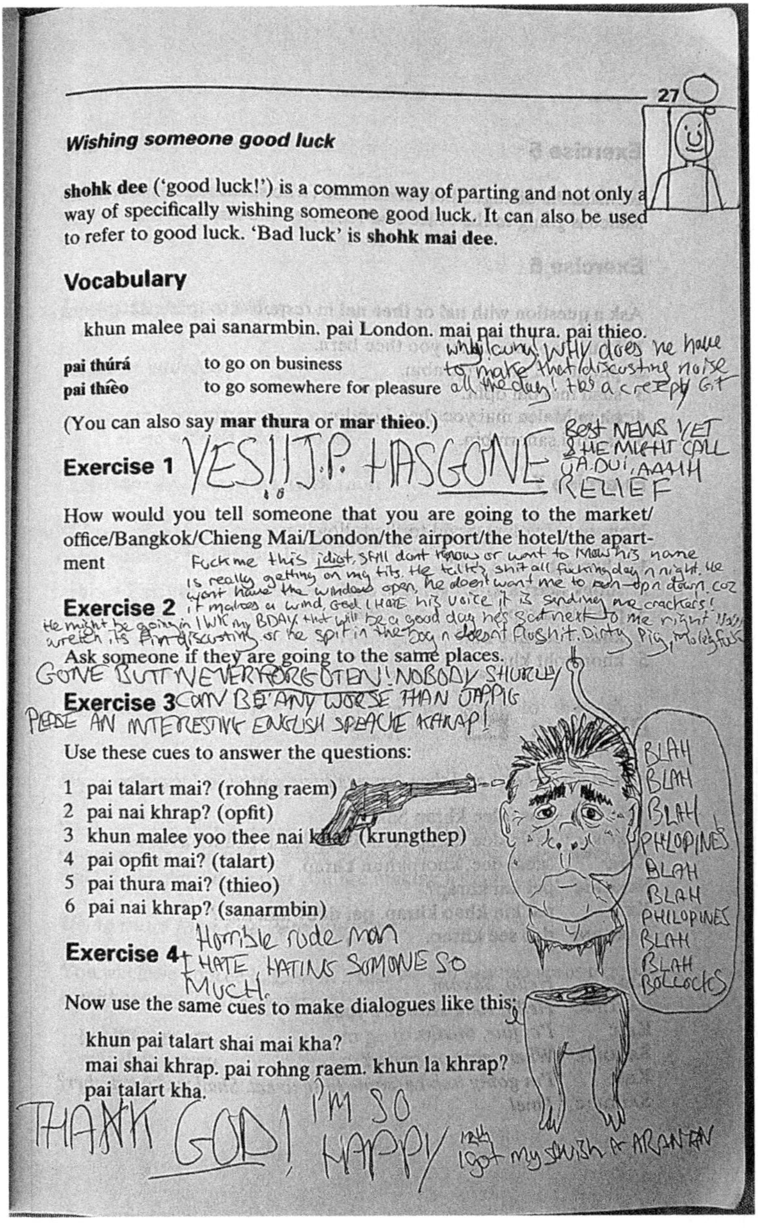

27

Wishing someone good luck

shohk dee ('good luck!') is a common way of parting and not only a way of specifically wishing someone good luck. It can also be used to refer to good luck. 'Bad luck' is **shohk mai dee**.

Vocabulary

khun malee pai sanarmbin. pai London. mai pai thura. pai thieo.

pai thúrá	to go on business
pai thîeo	to go somewhere for pleasure

(You can also say **mar thura** or **mar thieo**.)

Exercise 1

How would you tell someone that you are going to the market/office/Bangkok/Chieng Mai/London/the airport/the hotel/the apartment

Exercise 2

Ask someone if they are going to the same places.

Exercise 3

Use these cues to answer the questions:

1 pai talart mai? (rohng raem)
2 pai nai khrap? (opfit)
3 khun malee yoo thee nai kha? (krungthep)
4 pai opfit mai? (talart)
5 pai thura mai? (thieo)
6 pai nai khrap? (sanarmbin)

Exercise 4

Now use the same cues to make dialogues like this:

khun pai talart shai mai kha?
mai shai khrap. pai rohng raem. khun la khrap?
pai talart kha.

Mad Max

He also came from Vancouver and was caught carrying four kilos of meth hidden in his suitcase. Almost as soon he got into our humble abode, he was protesting his innocence.

"OH MY GOD... I can't believe I could be so stupid as to trust that man. He was just a customer in my hair salon that said he could do me a favour and would lend me his suitcase so I could come and visit my darling Japanese girlfriend."

He was visibly shaking and sobbing with the knowledge that this was the first day of the worst of times.
We carried on talking after the lights had dimmed; as long as you kept it down to a whisper it was excepted by all.

"I don't think the police upstairs believed me."

Neither did I.

"OK, Max, just tell me exactly what happened from the start."

As he went through his cover story, his eyes were all over the place, you could see his brain working overtime just to get the story right.

"Mate, stop right there. You must keep eye contact with me. If I was the inspector, I would think you were lying too."

I was quick to make it clear that he could be telling the truth, but his body language was clearly showing that he was lying.

Of course, he was full of shite just like the rest of us, but what else do you have when you're looking at ten years?

I think out of all the cases, only me and J.P. appeared to be coming clean.
Can people get set up?
Well, I'm sure it can happen.
Did I see any of them in the three months I was in the station? I highly doubt it.
And now, on to the next Mr. Innocent...

Claudia

Remember my advice - if you can call it that - on keeping a story simple?
Ladies and gentlemen, here is an example of the complete opposite.

I give you Claudia.

We all heard him before he was seen.
We were all just stewing over our downfalls when all of a sudden, there was all this commotion.

"I'M NOT ANSWERING ANY FECKING QUESTIONS UNTIL I GET A CIGARETTE."

"YOU DON'T KNOW WHO YOU'RE DEALING WITH, I'M WINNIE MANDELA'S MASSEUSE, I'M WELL KNOWN... AHHH, YOU'RE GANNA FECKING GET IT WHEN THEY FIND OUT WHAT'S HAPPENED TO ME."

There was a general feeling of 'who the fuck is this idiot?' amongst us.

"YOU FECKING SLANT-EYED BAASTARDS, NO WONDER YOU LOST THE WAR. THE ATOM BOMB WILL BE FECK ALL COMPARED TO WHAT HAPPENS WHEN MY PEOPLE FIND OUT WHAT'S HAPPENED TO ME"

"IT'S ALL A BLOODY FECKING SET UP. WHERE'S MY FECKING CIGARETTE?"

So you get the idea of what we had here.
We still hadn't seen him yet but the way he was going on about how he made suits for the Italian mafia –

"THE BLAADY CORSICAN MAFIA, NOT THE SILLY FECKERS YOU GET ON THE TV, THESE ARE THE REAL DEAL."

gave us all a mental picture of what to expect.
He continued saying how he was involved with Italian politicians and was a big deal in the business world.

So, you know when you hear someone's voice, and you start to get a visual idea of what you think they might look like in your head?
Well with everything that he was saying, I had this image of a tall, well-dressed gangster/businessman type bloke.
Hair all slicked back, well-groomed etc.
I was picturing a Dean Martin looking type of guy.

The door opened and in walked a five foot five, fat, balding bloke with the 'I'm not bald, I've got a ponytail' look complete with those Captain Kirk sideburns.

Just picture the comic book guy from the Simpsons.

"For fuck's sake."

I just shook my head.
I kinda felt sorry for him because in a way he **was** saying what we all thought when we first came in.
Surely, we did have rights, surely, we are allowed to have a bloody cigarette.

I never really met the bloke until many weeks later but I could hear him from his cell.
I was in cell number one and he was in cell number seven, but he was that loud I still got to hear his bullshit all the same.

He came in from Pretoria, South Africa, on some elaborate business deal and as well as being Winnie Mandela's masseuse and an Italian suit maker to the top brass, he was also a great white shark hunter.

He would go on about how he came to Japan to help them rebuild their economy (I guess he thought Japan was still on its knees after the war) but was set up...

"BY THE BLAADY KAFIRS."

So, as you can clearly see, he was just full of shit and he did everyone's head in.
Gee was in the next cell but one to him and became a representative for what the rest of us where thinking and would regularly tell him to

"SHUT THE FUCK UP."

His constant whining about how he had diabetes and how they (whoever the fuck 'they' were?) were trying to kill him and it was all part of the big set up because of course...
he was innocent.

Fuji

At 25-years-old, this young family man's life was to be crushed by attempting to smuggle in four kilos of meth. He came into our new world (cell) a few weeks before Christmas and thankfully fitted in well with this odd bunch of fuck-ups.

He was a kickboxer with shins of concrete so you knew he was for real, and we'd play a game where we would stand on one leg in front of each other and kick the other over for points or throw jabs at each other's shoulders also on a score system.
Basically anything that didn't actually mean hurting anyone but it passed the time.

When it was my days in court or a family member's birthday, Fuji would unselfishly give me his Valium to help take the edge off.

Hong Kong Ting Tong

He was another one who I heard about long before I met him. He was right down the other end of the station and from what I gathered via the the Narita grapevine, he was like a Chinese version of Claudia.
I remember Gee telling me,

"We've got a right Chinese nutjob down here."

He would witter on incessantly and couldn't speak a word of English or Japanese but was doing everyone's head in.
Ting Tong is Thai for someone who is crazy.
Not full-on mental but you know?
The kind of mental where you raise your eyebrows and do the international sign for nutjob (twirling your finger round next to your temple).
The sound of the phrase 'Ting Tong' explains it all really.

I met him on New Year's Eve when he got put into my cell while his cell was being searched.
As soon as he walked in I thought to myself,
'oh no, this is that Hong Kong Ting Tong from down the other end'.
We did the cagey 'Hello', and straightaway, he said,
" me no speak English,"
then started to do a kind of impression of an Orang-utan.
Me, Keeny, Max, and Fuji just looked at each other and burst out laughing.
He was a nutjob, but...he was also funny, and he was only in with us for one night.

I remember I was sorting my bed out and I kinda leant forward to adjust something and when I fell back onto my pillow, the fucker had nicked it and I banged my head against the wall.
Another time, he just started walking around the cell like a zombie and he had us all in stitches.

So, picture the scene:
I start the new year in a Japanese prison with a Chinese zombie nutjob, was this a sign of things to come?
I don't know what it is about nutjobs but I do kind of like them.
I remember seeing him a few weeks later after he had been sentenced. He was walking past my cell and he was a completely different man.
He looked entirely broken.
I gave him the thumbs up and said to him,
"You alright, mate?"
He just looked back at me and put all ten fingers up and then another two.
He'd been given 12 years and had the Ting Tong slapped right out of him.

Santa

Johan arrived on Christmas day from South Africa and after a body search, he was busted with 1.5 kilos of meth hidden in his underwear.

He was 55 years old but looked older with a big white beard and because he arrived at Christmas, he was given the name Santa.
He was put into the cell next door and straightaway, was asking lots of questions at the back window.

I always found it interesting and amusing I must say, watching how people act once they've been caught.
Santa couldn't go down the 'I had no idea I was smuggling drugs' route because they were in his underpants so he went with the good old 'if I didn't do it, the bad guys would kill my mother' routine.
All over a gambling debt of course.
I don't doubt for a second that the gambling bit was true but the rest sounded made up.

He was truly gutted that his elderly mother would have to get the news about her only son spending most likely the rest of **her** life in a Japanese prison, imagine living with that.

He, like Claudia, had every ailment under the sun and both of them were constantly harassing the guards for one thing or another and were driving everyone else nuts.

"Guard... guard... guard... come and assist me, I need more medicine. Guard... guard.... guard... let me out to see a doctor, I know my rights. Guard"... and so on.

Every fucking day.

"SHUT THE FUCK UP,"
said Gee and everyone else gave him a cheer.

This had become Gee's unofficial job now and he was the tannoy for what we were all thinking.
Gee had to put up with both of the whinging South Africans. He had one on each side of his cell and it was sending him crackers.

I tried talking to Santa on many occasions but it was pointless. He just loved a good whinge.
I'll give you a typical example of what these fuckers were like.

Santa had been pestering to be seen by a doctor for days so when they finally came to take him, he refused to go until he had his breakfast.
I couldn't believe it, and that's when I had a little pop at him.

"Johan, I've been helping you get this appointment for days and now you won't go because you might miss breakfast? Come on, for fuck's sakes mate, you'll most likely get some food somehow."

"I know my blaady rights just now."

"Oh, fuck off Santa."

That was my good Samaritan bit done.
I started to take the piss out of him and I stuck a pillow down the front of my boxers and was walking around saying,

"diplomatic immunity," "I know my rights," "I was set up by the fecking kaffirs!"

Everyone, and especially Max, was in hysterics and he got told off by the guards.
It was worth it though as this was the first time we'd had a really good laugh and let ourselves go.
It was a good release from the tension and all the crap that we

had to put up with.
You can't beat a good old giggle on.

Mr. Roy

Roy was half Japanese and half-Chinese and had flown in from New York where he'd been for a long weekend break with his boyfriend.
On the way back, he bought a watch on the plane duty free, but when he landed, he was arrested for credit card fraud and the poor bugger had no idea what had happened.

Unlike the rest of us, he was genuinely innocent and thankfully he did get off with it in the end, but only after a month in Narita and a week in Chiba.
This is where I got to bid him farewell and goodbye, as it turned out at our peril.
I don't think I can ever recall seeing someone so scared.

While in Narita, he was such a calming influence on all of us and because he has such a soft voice, everyone would be quiet when he spoke so that they could hear what he was saying.
He was in his early 30s but had a wisdom beyond his years and we all respected him to the point where we actually called him Mr. Roy.
He was in cell four which was pretty much dead centre of the block which was ideal, because when he would teach us Tai Chi and read from his Buddhist book, we could all hear him.

Meeting beautiful humans like him, beaming with positivity, would make such a difference on a crazy journey like this.
Not to everyone though, of course.
There are always those black holes of negativity that live to just suck all the positivity out of the world and want you to be as miserable as them.

Both of the racist, homophobic, South Africans were prime examples who said,
"The blaady pufffter was guilty and it was all an act."

Each to their own, I guess.

Cockney Ken

On the second day at pack up and wash time, I heard a London accent.
Wow.
I jumped up and went to the front bars to see an English fella who was just setting off back to his cell, which was right at the other end of the building (cell nine), so we never got chance to chat.

"Hey mate, where you from? I'm Ste from Lancashire."

"Well, fack me, I'm Ken from London, mate."

And that was all we got to say until the week after, when it clicked as to who he really was.

Rastaman

Now, I can't actually remember his name, but he was commonly known as Rastaman amongst our merry band of brothers.
He was your classic Jamaican-looking guy, Tall, skinny, with long dreadlocks, and he had made quite an impression on the local authorities.
When he arrived, there was a big commotion.
We could hear him kicking off, so he was put straight into the padded cell.

After a while, word had been passed down that he was some bigtime Yardie boss who had been caught in some kind of sting operation and it was a big deal.

After about three days, he was taken from the padded cell and was put into cell three which was next door but one to mine. As he walked past my cell, he was walking with a kinda tough guy swagger, proper giving it Mr. Billy big time.
I wasn't buying it.
It reminded me of Richard Pryor in the movie Stir Crazy when he was pretending to be a 'badass' and I couldn't help but smile and think,

fuck off, you having a laugh?

Being in cell one, everyone had to walk past our cell to get to theirs's so I had become like the doorman of the block and would try to give them words of encouragement.

"Alright, mate? Don't worry, it's not as bad as it looks here, you'll be alright."

After a while and a few lengthy discussions, he finally let his guard down.
It turned out that he wasn't the big Yardie boss man we all thought he was and as usual, the rumours were just bollocks. He was from Notting Hill and on the flight into Japan, had got absolutely hammered on brandy and went completely mental on the plane.

He told me how ashamed he was and that he must have shit himself on the plane, because when they tried to take him from the plane to the police van, he started to throw his own shit at the police.
All the commotion that we heard when he arrived at Narita was the police hosing him down then throwing him into the padded cell.

He was so embarrassed and was a nice guy really.
I couldn't help but take the piss out of him for his Richard Pryor Walk to the cell and he confessed that he was so scared he didn't know what to do so tried to play the part.
I told him he was a bad actor and should maybe be more of a Bob Marley than King Willy from Predator 2.

Day four: Pointless investigations.

I was slowly adjusting to my capture and downfall.
I still couldn't get my head around the idea of spending four to ten years of my life locked away from the world, but the wise folk in the cells reassured me that the embassy was wrong, so I chose to go with them.

I was more than happy to get out of the cell and go up to the interview room. I got the feeling that for myself and the interrogators, as far as cases go, this was easy-peasy.
I mean, I wasn't denying anything and compared to all the rest of the hardcore drug smugglers pleading innocence, my case was simple... until...

"Steven, who is this?"

What the actual fuck?

They were showing me that business card again.
The same one that the Iron lady from Chiba had been banging on about.

"I have no idea and don't get why it seems to be a big thing, what's the problem with it?"

I didn't have a Scooby Doo what they were on about.
There were that many dogs barking up so many wrong trees, this must have been the noisiest forest in Japan.
Well, it made no difference to me.
I was more than happy to waste time up here drinking coffee with a nice view.

'I wonder how often they clean these windows?'

Day 6

On my return to Chiba, I mentally prepared myself.
My conversations with Pier and Mr. Roy put me in the right frame of mind.

James was an Australian lad who was in cell nine at Narita and it wasn't until this day that I got to know him.
He was only 18 and was on a student's group trip to Japan.
He got a bit pissed up on the plane and when he got to the carousel, a random woman bent down to pick her bag up, so he made a massive fart noise just for a bit of a laugh.

He said the place was in stiches but the woman got so embarrassed, she went right over the top, going nuts and claiming that he'd smacked her on the backside.
So, the police got involved and that was him, ten days in jail then sent packing back home to Australia.

Yep, what a silly cow.

He told me the story on the bus and thankfully, we got put in the cell together.
He was only young but was a right big galoot of a lad, a real dead ringer for Jethro from The Beverly Hillbillies.
He cracked me up all morning, taking the piss out of everyone else in the cell and the guards.
We played eye spy.

James: " I spy with my little eye something beginning with C."

"Crack?"

"Naa"

"Curls?"

"Naa... but close."

I was always shit at this game, my sisters would always beat me, and it did my head in.

"Ok, I give in, you win. Go on, what is it?"

He then pointed to this big fat tattooed Yakuza guy that wouldn't shut up and shouted,
"CUNT."
The way he did it was so funny and most likely the Yakuza guy didn't know what a cunt meant, but it bloody well cracked me up, although I was thinking,
'shit, we might be kicking off here '
which made it even funnier.

He did impersonations of anyone in the cell that had a foible, and he had that goofy Jim Carey way about him when he did it.
He was really funny.
Even the food seemed better with him around. It's probably all in the head and also it wasn't as claustrophobic this time, so I felt ready to do battle with Margaret Hatchaa...bring it on.

My name was called out and off I went.
I'd told James all about this woman and what happened last time and as much as I appreciated his words of wisdom,

"FUCK THAT BITCH. DON'T LET EM GRIND YE DOWN, MATE,"

I just wish he hadn't said it so flipping loud.
Thankfully, there was no way she would have heard it.

"Cheers mate, good luck not getting bummed while I'm away."

As soon as I entered the room, I knew straight away who I was dealing with. It was the guy Kim had warned me about.
A small bald fella with big round rimmed glasses.
I sat down and was cuffed to the chair as standard.
I attempted to be polite and said,
"Kon ishi wa."
There was no response from him or the translator who looked just as intimidated as me.
It was really weird.

He didn't say anything for a good ten minutes.

He was just going through lots of papers and faffing and then he said...

"Kenneth Horsefield? How are you connected?"

"Is this the guy from the card I had in my wallet?"

"You know very well it is, and you know very well who **he** is. You have the same phone number in your phones so how could you not?"

He just fell short of adding an 'AHAAA' at the end.

"Really?...... Who?"

Now this got me thinking because I only had about 20 or so numbers in my phone, but he wouldn't give me any more information, he was waiting for me to trip myself up.

More mind games and then...

"EXPLAIN THIS?"

Whilst showing me a blown-up photo of the dead dove, poker chips, and money I'd taken in Brizvegas.
I was taken back a bit thinking,
'they can't be serious. What the hell is going on here?'

I just laughed and said,

"Well... It's a kinda joke."

"JOKE? HOW IS THIS FUNNY?" screamed specky.
I don't know why they had a translator because he never used him. In fact, it was like an insult to his English, which to be fair was very good, but he most certainly didn't get the English (or my) sense of humour.

I went through everything about why I just thought it would be a good photo, but he was having none of it.

Once again, they were barking up the wrong tree as it was all completely innocent, but I was fine with all his aggressive bullying tactics.

He was trying to use a power play of what they would or could do to me unless I told the truth.

At one point just to wind him up, I remembered the confusion with 'Maggie' over the phrase 'Reyt piss about' and decided I'd use this to throw a spanner in the works and give me a bit of power back.

With the knowledge that he'd have no idea what I was saying I looked him right in the eye and said…

"Reyt, ye specky four-eyed twat, you're giving it all the Billy big bollocks when in actual fact you're as far as comeback where the Geese go barefooted. I tried to get thi ta sit down and cut your sen a butt but what's gonna happen is that I'll punce thi up and down wi me stail nail boots like a football."

I got all that old Lancashire talk off Woz's Grandad and I never thought I'd be able to use it to confuse the fuck out of a Japanese interrogator.

While he was on the back foot trying to figure out what the fuck I was on about, I asked him what about the rest of the photos in the camera that show me bricklaying and working my bollocks off in the Queensland heat?

He had no answer to that so didn't even respond to me.

Next up was another little surprise I didn't see coming.
He had gone through my private investigator website.
It was very a basic description of the job, but for a laugh, I put in a well-known Pattaya bar girl phrase.

'Three-minute, three inch, three thousand. Easy-peasy, Japanesey.'

Well, explaining that one and with a female translator present was quite enjoyable, but all the while I knew that this wasn't going to make it better.
Quite the opposite, but to me it was worth it.

"Well, you see, the Thai girls say you have really small penises and that you ejaculate very quickly making it a very easy job. **and** they charge you three times the price of other foreigners."

He just stared back at me.

I just stared back at him and then raised my eyebrows and nodded.
It was almost like I could see his thoughts.

'YOU TWAT.'

I think it kind of worked though, because as it turned out, that was todays investigation done.
The next time I would go to Chiba it would be for the trial.

The plot thickens; Day 7
Back in Narita, and after a long day in the cell of doing nothing but worrying and attempting to read as a form of distraction, yet not getting past the first page without having a clue what I'd just read, I found that drawing was my best way to give the overthinking a rest.

I drew a big fantasy farmhouse where one day I might live. As it got to wash and brush your teeth time, the Cockney guy came for his turn, so we had a little chat.

"What you in for, mate?"

He took the now all too familiar long sigh and said,

"Three kilos of Ice. I've been set up, mate, by some cant in Sarf Afwica."

'Join the club', I thought.
So, that's John, Claudia, and now this guy, all flying in from Johannesburg, and all innocent.

"Whereabouts in London you from, mate?"

"East End but I've lived in Thailand... Pattaya for the last three years and I'm married to a Thai bird."

WELL FUCK ME SIDEWAYS.

This hit me like a ton of bricks...
This was Kenneth Horsfield.
Straightaway, I remembered meeting him with a few of my mates at a pool party on the dark side (an area of Pattaya known as the dark side because of the lack of lights and it sounded good. Nothing too seedy of course).
At that time, I was plastering stickers up everywhere for my PI job, and we were just chatting away and I told him of my new enterprise and he thought it was a great idea and gave me his business card.

That was it.
I never saw him again until here in Narita police station.

"Fuck me, mate, I'm from Pattaya too. I met you at a pool party once. We swapped cards and the investigators have been bugging me all week about it. I had no idea until now. WOW. I can't believe it. What are the chances of that?"

My mind went into overtime.
I presumed he was involved with my lot, and I started to check what I was going to say, thinking they could be listening in to everything.

"Naa, mate. I don't remember, if I'm honest, well yeah, maybe we did meet but..."

It was like someone had just slipped a finger up his arse.

He just stopped talking.

I could tell he was in shock, and he thought it was probably best to keep shtum.
He walked off with a million and one thoughts in his head and that gave **me** plenty to think about for the long-dreaded night ahead.
To be completely honest, at this point all I could think about was how this could affect me and my case.

On the eight day
God created an... imaginary Woz and Shannon Elizabeth (90s sex symbol from American Pie).

Yep, I needed someone to talk to on these long, lonely

nights so it might as well be my best mate and a fit bird that can play poker.

She was also a black belt in 'kick the fuck out of JP when he did his 'Phiiiiilliiiipines' drawl. Every time he was about to say it, she would emerge from the corner of the cell and cock her leg ready for the inevitable verbal vomit and boot him right in his big, fat, pig head.

Woz would acknowledge this with the good old Stan Laurel 'you deserved that' nod.

Woz would always go on at me for being the bellend that I was but Shannon would back me up and tell Woz to

'shut up and leave him alone'.

She could see that I was down and would cheer me up by flashing me her tits.

Cheers for that, Shannon.

So, the three of us discussed the new Ken development.
A few things twigged with me right away.
I told Shannon and Woz,

'Big Gary was there at the pool party, as was Trevor, the guy he sent to Johannesburg. Now, if you remember, Pete told Gary to get Trevor on the next flight back or there would be consequences'.
Woz spat back,

'Like shite he did. I told you not to get involved with that lot.'
I continued,

'SOOO, Gaz must have sent Ken behind our backs and maybe, somehow, Abbie found out and quite possibly grassed Ken up and he got caught. Gaz knew damn well that me and Jake were on the way to Japan, and out of spite dropped us, or me, right in the shit.'
Shannon gave me a look of sympathy and said,

'Oh Stevie, it all seems fairly cut and dried here buddy. That Gaz is a piece of work.'

To this day, I don't know for sure what actually happened, but that was, and is, the most likely way it happened.
I mean, Ken got caught in Japan and then three days later, the Japs were waiting for me.
Coincidence?
Paranoia?
I'm not sure about those words but there was one word that was becoming more apparent.

SCHIZOPHRENIA.

I mean, I have had some bizarre coincidences in the past and sometimes, it has turned out that I was right to be paranoid, but the fact that I was definitely set up and it wasn't just a random bag check favoured treachery.

So, you're all part of this now reader...what do you think?

Again, this was always my choice and no matter why it went wrong, something like that was always on the cards.
No honour amongst thieves and drug smugglers as it turns out.

Back upstairs for more cosy chats and straightaway, I told them that I now knew who Ken Horsfield was and how I had got hold of his card.
I explained that he was downstairs and that I had just met him and it jogged my memory, so now that we were all on the same page, I could explain everything.
Well... except for the truth.
I told them how we had just innocently swapped cards and that I vaguely remember doing this but he didn't remember me. He bloody well did remember me but was sticking to his

story that he couldn't remember me.
No need for a web of lies if you simply can't remember anything.

This didn't go down too well, but it really wasn't that far from the truth, so I was OK with whatever they asked me. You ready for another spanner in the works?

"Gary Bolton? Does that name ring any bells?"

"No,"
I replied while thinking,
'Oh, shit, that must be Big Gaz's real name.'

They continued,
"Because Kenneth Horsfield had written that name and telephone number on his plane ticket, and that number is in in your phone. Please explain that, Mr. Beattie?"

"Well, I guess we must know a lot of the same people in Pattaya. I only know him as Big Gaz." (Which was true).

They kept going over the same shite and from different angles but it always ended up in the same 'fuck knows' cul-de-sac.
I could feel that everything was aimed at catching Ken's lies out, because they'd pretty much gone as far as they could with me.
I went back to Chiba for one more formality round with prosecutor specky.
Him trying to catch me out and me sticking to a simple 'ignorance is bliss' story.

It worked, and the dreaded passport stamp was never found, so now it was just a waiting game until my day in court.

A day in the life

So, it turns out me and Paul McCartney have a few things in common.
We both have ties to Liverpool, we're both musicians, and we've both been banged up in Narita cells for smuggling cannabis.
I did recall something about him getting caught with a bit of personal use but it was actually 219 grams and if it wasn't for being who he was, he could have been sentenced to up to seven years in prison.

For those of you who enjoy diving down conspiracy rabbit holes, there are rumours that Yoko Ono got him out.
Also, there are rumours that Yoko Ono tipped off the authorities and got him nicked and that's rumours for ye.

Dad's army

Once the guards found out I was English and that my dad was from Liverpool, they loved it.
After all these years, the Beatles were still huge and one of the guards would bring CDs to play all day ranging, from The Beatles to Blur, Oasis back to The Stones, and everything else in-between that was British.

These tantos (guards) were a comical lot.
They were very reminiscent of the old TV show, Dad's Army.
Most of them were over 60, but there was one young lad in his

mid-20s who seemed a bit, well ye know...funny.

As in 'funny in the head'.

A bit thick.

To be honest, he was a top lad and like most of them would do whatever they could to help you.

The one that brought the CDs was amazed when I told him,

"Ye know the song, 'A Day in The Life' by The Beatles and that bit where Lennon mentions Blackburn in Lancashire? Well, that's where I'm from."
He was really impressed and got me a cup of tea.
What a nice man.

The main tanto had a look of Spock from Star Trek, shorter, but with a bigger head.
Not that I'd met Leonard Nimoy or that I know how tall he was.
It's just an educated guess.
He tried to be the big strict boss and every now and then, he pulled it off.
He had an incredibly deep voice like Windsor Davies (Battery Sergeant Major Williams) from 'It Ain't Half Hot Mum' (another UK army-based comedy).
That said, he was a kind-hearted soul that must have seen countless people who were at the start of a very long and bad period in their lives.

There was a lot of stress within these walls, all mixed in with worry, blame, and the unknown, which was an absolute killer to us all.
The unknown would be quite the nemesis as the days would turn into weeks, would turn into months...

I still hadn't seen a doctor; every time he came to the station, I was either upstairs getting interviewed or off to be interrogated at Chiba.
I had developed a toothache, but the tantos helped me book the dentist.

I hadn't had a proper crap in all the time I was there and I was losing a lot of weight.
I was constantly hungry.
I was exercising as much as I could whilst being careful not to burn too many calories so as not to starve myself.
Just getting through the first week felt like an achievement in itself.

I'd hardly slept and was getting exhausted; the sleep deprivation and all the stress makes for a long 24 hours and as the days go by, time blurs into an eternity.
Thankfully, they had a small library and books would be brought via a portable trolley.
We could take out three books per day but they had to be returned in the evening so you couldn't guarantee that you'd be able to get the same book back the next day to continue reading it because someone else might pick it up before you.

We got pens passed to us through the food hatch, but I didn't get any paper for a while so had to write in the three books I came with:

'Stop Smoking the Easy Way' by Alan Carr (highly recommended),
my 'Learn to Speak Thai' book, and 'Guns, Germs and Steel' by Jerad Diamond.
I'd bought it in Goa but it was a hard read, very interesting, but in this place, I struggled with deep thought.

I was still trying to adjust mentally to my new life here and the new life that lay ahead of me.
I figured that things were going to get a lot worse, so my

thoughts were kinda skittish and it was hard to focus.
A simple read that I could just float along with was the best way to pass the time.
It became a great joy to get into a good book. I'd never been a big reader but by the time I was released back into the world I'd read hundreds of them.

There was one particular book that was an absolute lifesaver and not one that I would ever read in normal circumstances.

Jackie Collins' 'Lucky's revenge'.

My first wank in the bogs when everyone was asleep...

I think...

I hope.

Prisoners Abroad

Henry from the embassy introduced me to a monthly magazine from a UK-based charity called 'Prisoners Abroad'. It was such a comfort to read about people who were in a similar situation to me and read about their stories. Stories that came from all over the world and many were in a lot harsher conditions than those I was in...for now.
The magazine has sections on art, poetry, and letters, and at the back, they had some basic yoga positions and ways to relieve your stress.
It was a godsend; no other country produced a magazine like this and I did feel a sense of pride that I was from the UK. Though I'm not sure that the UK would be as proud of me in my present climate, so I'd have to make amends and be the best I could be. I'd always share the magazine with the others as I knew how much it helped.

I really looked forward to a new one coming every month.
Japan is the only country in the world that won't allow prisoners to have anything sent to them but once free, I went to London and did a day's filming to raise money for their charity event and I did the artwork for their brochure and tickets.
I will never forget how grateful I was for their help.
Oh, and I got second in a poker comp for £550…see…
Karma.

You might be thinking it's not so bad here in Narita.
I seem to be painting a nice little picture of how pleasant it was with the nice, friendly guards and half-decent food.
I was warm, sat down chilling, reading, writing, and drawing away listening to my favourite music all day.
This is true.
It wasn't so bad that way, but the long, long days and nights were a constant battle to keep away the torturous thoughts of dread and worry of what was to come.
I was constantly hearing all the conflicting rumours.
There was always someone complaining about silly things.
God knows how these types would get on in the hell that was to come.

Time was dragging on and I just wanted it to be all over with. I was torturing myself with worry and constantly fighting off the creeping negativity but yet realising not to hang on to some kind of ridiculous hope with the sentencing like I could just somehow get lucky with the judge having a good day or the war on cannabis stopping.

Everything was starting to bug me, especially Mad Max because he would lie on his side and would have me standing on his knees to help massage out his constant pain, but he would moan out loud like he was getting bummed.
Now at first, we all just laughed at it but after a while it got too

weird and I refused to do it unless he could keep quiet or at the very least tone down the homoerotic wailings.

Max's story

He was a hairdresser from Tehran, just living a normal, everyday life.
Then one day a random guy from some political group came into his salon wanting to promote his organization, but Max didn't want anything to do with it.
He loved the arts and had no interest in politics.
The guy left leaving behind a leaflet, and max thought that was the end of it but all the while he was being watched by the authorities.

The day after the Iranian army came in and took Max in for questioning. Max had no political affiliations; he was just an innocent hairdresser so wasn't the least bit worried.

A year later, after almost being tortured to death he didn't have the same faith that his innocence would protect him from his countries judicial system.
He was held in a cell which was just a small, concrete box.
It was completely blacked out and he was unable to stand or stretch out his limbs.
He would be taken out only to be put into a bigger cell, where he was stripped naked, hung upside down and beaten with sticks on his back, legs and the soles of his feet, until he was unconscious.
The beatings left him virtually crippled, and heavily scarred.
He told me,

"I confessed and told them everything that they wanted to hear even though I didn't know what I was saying."

After six months of torture, they must have realised he knew nothing and was just blurting out whatever would make them stop.

After over a year in a low security prison there was a riot and a few of the prisoners including Max took this opportunity to escape.
He then had one hell of a journey taking the old silk road (hippy trail) over the Zagros Mountain range to avoid the military. His destination was Istanbul and If you look on the map you will see this is quite some feat, especially with the condition his legs were in, but he knew that once across the border, he was a free man.

He claimed asylum in Turkey and there his fortune changed and with his newfound luck, he ended up getting to Vancouver, Canada where he settled for the last 20 years.

Max had a peculiar trait where he would tell people he was fifty years old when in actual fact he was only forty.
Now, most people when they lie about their age tend to knock years off and pretend they are younger than they are, so I don't know if he did this to bolster his self-esteem (he was only five foot two inches which wouldn't help) because people would say things like,

"Oh, you look really well for your age "
and he would be quite pleased with that and say.

"You want to see me with my hair piece on, I look thirty!"

I don't know why the guards confiscated his "syrup".
It wasn't as though he was going to beat anyone to death with it, but it really did his head in, and he begged to get it back.

"Please, please I will need it for my court case, it makes me look more distinguished!"

I could visualise him with his "rug" on, and totally understood where he was coming from.

He was tanned all over except for the white chrome dome and He just looked like a reyt daft slap head.

I knew that this time he was as guilty Hell, but he was a good man and most certainly didn't deserve to be put through his treatment in Tehran.

Every day at three pm we would get a Tea break.
Not that it was breaking anything up other than the monotony of the day, but it was a welcome little treat.
It was called Hoi Cha, which was basically, one green leaf Tea bag in a huge kettle. It would always be just shy of lukewarm and to even mention the word flavour in this description just doesn't seem right.
I told them we had a similar drink in England called "Lukewarm piss".

Every day Max would ask for extra and made sure they filled it up to the top, but they couldn't understand what he meant so he asked Keeny to teach him what "fill up" is in Japanese.

Now, full in Japanese is "ippai" but every bloody day he would say "oppai" which means big tits!
Me, Keeny and Fuji would laugh our heads off every time he said it wrong.
It was a relief to have Max instead of the retching JP for the upcoming festive season.

Being in prison at Christmas was the worst of times for me due to the fact that my second son was born on the 23rd of December, and it would absolutely kill me.
New year's would be the same kind of torture with the dreaded thought of how many new year's I'd have to spend in there.

Judgement day

January the 16th, 2009 was my first Saiban (trial).
I felt as good as I could about how the investigation went.
I really do think they thought it was my first time and the dodgy passport was never detected.
Of course, the Cockney Ken thing didn't help but it never came up on the day. Fuji had saved up his Valium for me, so I had four 10mg tablets to get me through the day.
I don't know whether it was due to all the stress, but it didn't feel like they worked.

I was the only one on the police minibus and we arrived at court for 1 p.m. On my way there, all I could do was hope for the best.
One?
Two?
I'd take three years at that point in time.

The courtroom was quite grand and reminded me of the old courtroom dramas (such as Crown Court on UK TV) with the wooden panels everywhere, and as I look back now, I can't help but feel like there were three judges with them daft white wigs on, but maybe the Valium did work after all.

My blinking twat of a lawyer seemed to represent me fairly well as it was all being translated for me.
I never got to say anything, and in all, it probably only took about an hour to pass judgement.

So, here was the verdict.

Seven years and a four million yen fine.

"Do you have anything to say Mr Beattie?"

I'm still feeling the shock to this day from hearing the translator say it.

Keeny had drilled into me that no matter what sentence I got, I had to say sorry in Japanese. I had conditioned myself and was mentally prepared for this day but I kinda froze as my head couldn't get past the words.

"SEVEN YEARS"

I forgot how to say sorry in Japanese (Gomen Nasia).

I knew it ended in 'ia' but in my state of shock, I blurted out

"upai."

Oh my God, I just said big tits to a Japanese judge!

Mad bloody Max!
As soon as I said it, I realised I'd got it wrong, but fortunately I'd kind of mumbled it so it wasn't as bad as it sounds and they asked me to repeat it.
I just said,

"My sensei has been teaching me how to say sorry but on hearing how bad the sentence is, it's completely thrown me and I can't remember the right word so all I can say in my language is I'm truly sorry."

I feel in some ways, that came across more sincere.

I was gutted to say the least and was in a state of shock, I mean what did that actually mean?
I knew I would go back within the next two weeks to get the final sentence and it would be discounted, but starting at seven was not good, to say the least.

When I got back to Narita, everyone was gobsmacked but they all tried to make me feel better in any way that they could, but there were lots of long silences as the ice carriers were most likely thinking,

'fuck, well, what are we gonna get?'

On the 19th, I got my first letter off Woz and some old photos of us and that cheered me up no end.

The next two weeks dragged more than ever, and the 23rd of January was my little girl's 11th birthday, which really rubbed salt into the wounds.

It's incredibly hard to process all the emotions stirred up by this absolute calamity of a fuck up that I was in, but I still tried to turn it into a positive outcome. At least it wasn't a ten-year sentence and that it wasn't Ice that I was caught with like the rest of the poor sods.

Almost every day, there would be someone coming back from his first or second Saiban and all of them had it way worse than me.

I also got a letter off my brother telling me that his wife's father in the Philippines had been murdered by her mother. She'd hired two goofballs to shoot him for a poxy 2k insurance job, but it looked well suss and the insurance company smelt a rat and they never got paid.
The two so-called hitmen took over the little family shop and I mean little, it was about the same size as my prison cell.

So, in the end, to cut a long story short, and so as not to incriminate anyone else, they ended up shot dead as well. One in the actual shop and the other later who went on the run disguised as a ladyboy.
The wife (mother) got away with it all.

So, compared to what they were going through, my little mishap didn't feel as bad... ish.

FINAL VERDICT

February 4th, 2009 was the big day.

Was there any chance I could get a massive reduction?
Yes.

Was it realistic I could get a massive reduction?
No.

The first Saiban had to deal with the details of the case. The who, where, what, And how?

The second Saiban one was a very short and to the point experience.

"Mr Steven Beattie, your sentence for attempting to smuggle 1.96 kg of Cannabis resin to Japan is..."

"5 years, 100 days and a fine of 1 million yen."

"Do you have anything to say Mr Beattie?"

To be continued…

To the smokers I have failed to cure,
I hope it will help them to get free

And to Sid Sutton

But most of all to Joyce Mum X
BEATTIE Sorry mum mis 1/60
         your the best X
         I Love you

BANGO
Part II:
A Prisoners Tale

Fuchu or as I liked to call it Fucku, is known as one of the strictest and most secretive prisons in the world.

I had a simple plan,
keep my head down,
don't get involved with the Yakuza,
respect the guards, respect the system.

As you may have gathered, things don't always go to plan and I would soon come to realize that the Japanese are the masters of head fuckery.

BIG TROUBLE IN TOKYO

Banged up Abroad or Locked up Abroad as it's called in America was made for National geographic by the production company Raw T.V.

I did a podcast with the YouTuber and fellow ex-convict Shaun Attwood, and Raw T.V. contacted me via Shaun.

The first question that everyone always asks me is, how much did I get paid?

I went down to London and stayed for three nights and did two long, solid days of filming.
They couldn't do enough for me, but it was gruelling, and by the end of the filming I was exhausted and just laid back on the bed thinking,

'thank God that's over with'.

It was a similar feeling as in Okinawa after my first run, although now I was feeling regret rather than relief.

I knew they could twist and shape any version of the story that they wanted but fair play to them, they stayed true to their word, and it came out very close to what I hoped for.

Oh sorry, do you still want to know how much I got?
Of course you do ye nosey bastard.
£1000 + three nights in a fancy London hotel all expenses paid.

I watched it for the first time when it aired in Pattaya with a certain friend of mine. It's a bizarre feeling watching this part of my life on T.V. in the place where it all started.

When it finished, I turned to my mate and we both had tears in our eyes, we called each other soft cunts and he said.

" They could have put the bit in with me and the Delhi police van at the hotel!"

I once read,
"Never start or finish a story with profanities."

"bollocks"

Check out our Youtube channel,
https://www.youtube.com/@thestewozshow7042

https://youtu.be/yNHmxCw7jDk?si=B3j1zg4uuEemDwx1

https://youtu.be/t85vg-vsLvg?si=7Rpg8xt7suN6oYyN

For more information contact thesteandwozshow@gmail.com.

Printed in Dunstable, United Kingdom